Sean Brunton is a writer, journalist and barrister.
He lives in Somerset with his family.

Pippa.

For your honest
effort in caring for
Steve.

Sean x

To my Mother and to my Father:
true British heroes both.

Sean Brunton

SIX OF THE BEST

A Pantheon of Great British Heroes

AUSTIN MACAULEY PUBLISHERS™

LONDON • CAMBRIDGE • NEW YORK • SHARJAH

A CIP catalogue record for this title is available from the British Library.

ISBN 9781398429024 (Paperback)
ISBN 9781398429031 (ePub e-book)

www.austinmacauley.com

First Published 2021
Austin Macauley Publishers Ltd
1 Canada Square
Canary Wharf
London E14 5AA

Acknowledgments

I would like to thank my wife Erica for her encouragement, balance and patience when listening to me, reading my drafts and helping me to use a computer. And for her kindness, tolerance and love.

I would like to thank my children Callum, Millie and Rory for their criticisms, irreverence and general good-humour.

I would like to thank my parents and my brother for their constructive criticisms and support.

I would like to thank my various history teachers at Oundle School for their excellent, memorable and often hilarious lessons: Alan Midgley, Ron Mather and 'Dinky' Sharp.

And I would like to thank those few friends who ever actually bothered to read, critique or correct the drafts I sent them.

Chapters

Introduction
No More Heroes?

OUR LAND IS governed by leaders who almost never fail to disappoint. Our lives are driven by insatiable commerce and technological obsession. Our societies are riven with conflicting views of how we ought to behave and how our history should be remembered, celebrated or erased. Our spirituality has been relegated to the fringes of society. In times as divisive, selfish and superficial as these, the need to find a hero and to speak of acts of heroism is irrepressible.

And so we struggle, somewhat desperately, to foist the mantle of 'hero' upon our sportsmen, so that Kane, Wilkinson and Murray at their finest are passed off as modern-day gladiators or living-room legends for doing little more than the swinging of a racket or the kicking of a ball. And for a while they struggle manfully under their burdens, until the inevitable injury, scandal or plain loss-of-form knocks them from their podium and cruelly exposes them to ridicule by the very people who were so desperate to worship them in the first place.

Such is the inherent need for hero-figures to lift our spirits from the triviality, political correctness and bureaucracy of modern Britain, that the media has become obsessed with celebrity, wealth and beauty. But these are not worthy substitutes for heroes nor for noble or truly

11

brave deeds. They are tawdry and distasteful diversions: eye candy to brighten the bleak prospect before us.

For a real hero is one who exhibits extraordinary bravery and spirit. One who is blessed with some superhuman ability or who, by strength of character, steels himself to behave as if he is so blessed. One who, by leadership and nobility and sheer daring can cheat the odds at a personal or national level, for himself or for others. And one whose acts were so genuinely magnificent that they endure and evolve in legend many years after the heroic bones lie buried. A modern-day hero is a tall order.

But perhaps that is no bad thing. It might be said that a nation which has need of a hero-figure must be lacking in self-confidence: must be desperate for some form of salvation or recognition; or is simply needy for some sense of direction or justification to release it from its troubles. Certainly, heroes and heroic acts often arise from times of crisis: 'Cometh the hour, cometh the man' and all that.

It was the constant tribal warfare of the Ancient Greeks which spawned their pantheon of hero demi-gods. The Vikings with their insatiable appetite for foreign invasions found solace in their own Norse heroes. And medieval Europe's scramble for power and riches created its own brand of swashbuckling chivalric heroes. All of them an elegant subterfuge to divert the minds of the people from the grim reality of life and death in more primitive socie-ties. A sugar-coating to disguise the bitter pill of history. If religion was the opium of the people, then heroic legend was the Carling Black Label of the working man. It deceives as it inspires.

In the Middle Ages, it was the knights in shining armour who did the job. Over the Napoleonic period, it was our great military commanders who came up with the goods. In the last century, the apocalyptic World Wars forged a new breed of hero and cast them unwillingly into history; the desperate, plucky and frequently tragic 'British Bull-dogs' who have defined our national character ever since.

If the horror, bloodshed and iniquity of previous centuries are the price a nation has to pay for its real heroes, then there are likely to be few takers in the 21st century. For all our protest and posturing, very few are prepared to make the ultimate sacrifice for some noble end. And yet that yearning still smoulders.

Whether it feeds on the creeping anxiety arising from global terrorism, breeds in the petty dissatisfactions of our increasingly isolated lives or rides upon the high-horse of outrage and helplessness with which we watch the destruction of our planet: it smoulders on. As we crumple our celebrity-infested newspapers into the fireplace or sit suffocating in our own traffic jams, we know we deserve better.

Great Britons deserve great heroes, not manufactured myths nor tinsel-town trash. And if we pause for a minute and think beyond the chat shows and the chat rooms, then we find them scattered through our nation's rich history in abundance.

'Unhappy is the land that needs a hero', or 'Unhappy is the land that breeds no hero'? So posed the poet, Bertolt Brecht. He somewhat bitterly favoured the former. But there again, as a German Marxist who lived through both World Wars, I suppose you can't really blame him.

So, whether bred, wanted or needed by these Isles, here are half-a-dozen men who have, according to the customs and norms of their age, conducted their lives in a manner which can best be described as heroic. Not necessarily worthy nor considerate; not always virtuous nor even particularly nice. But heroic giants nevertheless, and I challenge any other nation to assemble such an inspirational and defiant pantheon. I give you Six of the Best...

Richard I
Lionheart

RICHARD, 'COEUR DE Lion', Duke of Normandy and King of England, was a ruthless warlord and charismatic leader of men. He could allegedly sever an iron bar with one blow of his Great Sword, yet he was also a poet and, despite a number of notable lapses, the epitome of the chivalric knight. He battled his own father for the crown of England, abandoned his wife and put thousands of his prisoners to the sword. But he was also respectful of those enemies he thought worthy and was capable of acts of great mercy. As with many true heroes, he was a man of deep contradictions and one who has polarised opinion both at the time and ever since. As Sellar and Yeatman so neatly parodied in *1066 And All That*, 'Richard I was a hairy king with a lion's heart.' Rather more complimentary was the Syrian historian, Ali Ibn al-Athir who when travelling with Saladin's army wrote of Richard, 'His courage, cunning, energy and patience made him the most remarkable man of his time.'

Richard, third legitimate son of Henry II and great-great-grandson of William the Conqueror, was born in 1157 into a feuding dynastic Europe of Byzantine political complexity. Although born in Oxford in 1157 and spending his early childhood in England, at the age of eight he was sent abroad to take his place at the heart of the new Plantagenet-Angevin empire: a vast Anglo-French kingdom carefully fashioned from marriage, treaty and warfare. Thereafter, he spent almost his entire life away from England: either campaigning, on crusade or in captivity. His adolescence is obscure, but certainly by 1173, as the 16-year-old Count of Poitou, he had already become a military commander to be reckoned with.

Henry II had divided his French territorial possessions between his three oldest surviving heirs, leading to decades of internecine wars between them, their rebellious barons and their neighbours. Indeed, so bitter had the in-fighting become that at one point, Henry had taken his own wife, Eleanor of Aquitaine, as a prisoner. In those ferocious civil wars, so aggressive had Richard been in subduing and punishing his enemies and so tactically adept had he become, that when he laid siege to the seemingly impregnable Castillon sur Argen in 1175, aged 18, he managed to batter it into submission in just two months. At the Château de Taillebourg, four years later, a similar capitulation only took two days.

His sobriquet of 'Lionheart' seems to have emerged at about this time, and his reputation as a military commander was growing fast.

For the next decade or so Richard was busy securing his own power-base in Aquitaine, whilst also expanding his sphere of influence. Then, when his older brother Henry unexpectedly pre-deceased him, despite Richard being once more at War with his own father, King Henry rightly, but perhaps somewhat surprisingly, named Richard as his heir. A victory of legitimacy over popularity. In fact, only two days after being defeated by his 31-year-old son at the Battle of Ballans in July 1189, Henry died and Richard duly became King of England: crowned at Westminster Abbey on the 3rd September of that year.

Portrait of Richard (from Cassell's Illustrated History of England, *1865)*

Richard now took his place at the Top Table of a Europe obsessed with the idea of regaining Christian control of the Holy Lands generally and of the venerated city of Jerusalem in particular. Indeed, he and the other leaders of Christendom were incited by the Pope himself to 'Take the Cross'. Allegedly fulfilling a promise to his dying father and swearing to renounce his former brutality, Richard quickly set about organising the Third Crusade and beating a path to the walls of the Holy City of Jerusalem. Which, by modern standards may seem a somewhat contradictory pair of ambitions. In any event, such was the mistrust between him and Philip II, King of France, that they made a pact to go on the Third Crusade together, to prevent each other usurping the other's position at home whilst their back was turned...

It was with great difficulty that Richard was initially able to absent himself from his anarchic French territories at all. After all, the Angevin Empire stretched from the River Tweed to the Pyrenees and included parts of Wales, Ireland and over half of modern-day France, almost all of which was in a state of insurrection. But having finally done so in the summer of 1190, he found that things did not go smoothly.

En route to Palestine, initially he was diverted to Sicily to throw his weight behind a family dispute. His aunt, the recently widowed Queen of Sicily, had been imprisoned and deprived of her inheritance. Understandably, Richard had felt it necessary to intervene; which he certainly did, by attacking, capturing, looting and then burning the city of Messina. He then encamped there until his demands were met, which, within six months of arriving on the island, they were. 'Job done' and having finally once more set sail, his fleet was then scattered by storms and, on the 1st of May 1191, some of his ships, including both his treasure ship and the ship carrying his sister and his fiancée, Berengaria of Navarre, were shipwrecked on the island of Cyprus. When they were taken prisoner and the treasure seized by the Cypriot emperor, Richard invaded and, within barely a month, took the entire island by force. Having captured the emperor, he swore not to put him in irons; and so he secured him in chains of silver instead! He thereby not only rescued his fleet, treasure and his sister and fiancée, but he also annexed Cyprus as an essential harbour from which to re-supply his Crusade. Indeed, Cyprus remained a Christian bastion until the famous sea battle of Lepanto in 1571, nearly 400 years later. But, within days of being appointed Lord of Cyprus, Richard was off, never to set foot there again. He had stayed on the island just long enough to marry his betrothed. But, other than taking Berengaria with him for the start of the Third

Crusade, she was soon sent back to France and they barely ever saw each other again. By our contemporary standards, it was neither much of a honeymoon, nor much of a marriage.

Meanwhile, as the self-appointed head of a European alliance, on arrival at Acre in the Holy Land on the 8th of June 1191 he immediately confronted the Turk rulers of Palestine and particularly the Prince who was to become his nemesis: Saladin. Richard's stature is defined by his rivalry with that equally revered Muslim commander. The aura surrounding both men is rooted in the unquestionable respect these adversaries had for each other. Saladin, an aristocratic and highly educated fighting man, would send baskets of fresh fruit to refresh Richard when he struggled in the desert heat, observing that 'never have we had to face a bolder or more subtle opponent'. For his part, Richard knighted Saladin's nephew for his courage on the field of battle. The two commanders, the Christian and the Muslim, were fêted as examples of noble chivalry throughout medieval Europe.

That knightly hypocrisy, allying genteel pilgrim with armour-clad butcher, reached its epitome with Richard. Indeed, it was Richard who, seeking to protect his soldiers and to swell their hearts with religious zeal, first adopted St George as the patron saint of England. A heavenly cloak to conceal very earthly objectives. It was an inspired device. That red cross upon a white background has been the talismanic symbol of English pride, power and self-belief on both the battlefield and the sports field ever since. Likewise, the 'three lions passant guardant', so familiar to us on the breast of all England football jerseys, was first adopted by Richard and, along with the motto '*Dieu et mon droit*', constitutes the Royal Arms of England to this day.

Within five weeks of arriving, the city of Acre, which had hitherto withstood a two-year siege, fell to the English King.

Even when Richard had been suffering severely from scurvy, he had insisted upon using his crossbow to pick off the Turkish guards from high on the castle walls, as he lay on his stretcher. The routing of the Muslim army at Arsuff followed in September 1191.

Next came victory at the Battle of Jaffa. As an increasingly despondent Turkish chronicler admitted in his diary:

'The King of England, lance in hand, rode along the whole length of our army from right to left and not one of our soldiers left rank to attack him. The Sultan was wrath thereat and left the battlefield in anger.'

There is this said of Richard's exploits as he came to relieve the garrison at Jaffa:

'With no armour on his legs, he threw himself into the sea first... and fought himself powerfully onto dry land.'

*A somewhat fanciful depiction of the Battle of Arsuff
by Gustave Doré*

Perhaps the ultimate praise comes from the revered contemporary scholar, Ibn Shaddad who, when writing Saladin's biography in 1220, recorded this of Richard:

> 'See the cunning of this accursed man! To obtain his ends he would first employ force and then smooth words…God alone could protect the Muslims against his wiles. We never had to face a craftier or a bolder enemy.'

But it was not chivalry, nor subtlety which dictated Richard's most nefarious deed. Impatient with the Turks' apparent reluctance to finally come to terms after Richard's successful siege of Acre and wanting to press on without the burden of so many prisoners of war, he put 2,700 Turkish hostages to the sword in July 1191 in the infamous massacre of Ayyadieh. Hardly his finest hour. It is chilling testament to his reputation as a ruthless soldier living in unforgiving times. It is also an uncomfortable reminder that the religious promise of heavenly salvation for the slaughter of non-believers is no 21st-century phenomenon.

15th-century French depiction of the massacre of Ayyadieh

However, despite many further bloody encounters with Saladin, these two great military leaders, perhaps because of their mutual respect, were finally both able to emerge from the inconclusive Third Crusade with pride intact. Although Richard's army came close enough to Jerusalem to actually stare up at its sacred walls, dissension within the Crusaders' ranks meant that no siege was ever commenced and a treaty was finally thrashed out instead. Saladin retained control of Jerusalem and the majority of the Holy Land. However, he recognised Richard's territorial gains in the region and granted him access to Jerusalem for Christian pilgrims. As an exercise in compromise and pragmatic statesmanship, it still stands as an instructive example of the peace process in a troubled land.

But Richard's statesmanship with his fellow Europeans had not been so successful, largely on account of his opportunistic and forceful occupation of Cyprus en route. Soon after arriving in Palestine he had argued with and then shamed Duke Leopold of Austria by having the Duke's banners cast into the moat at Acre by the English soldiers, causing Leopold to return home in something of a sulk. Shortly after, Richard's uneasy alliance with the French King also floundered and Richard was left in Palestine without allies.

By now it was October 1192 and Richard had been away from Europe for over two years. With the European Princes working against him and to prevent the collapse of his kingdom at the hands of both the French King and his own treacherous brother John, Richard had little choice but to leave Palestine.

But, crossing the Mediterranean, he was shipwrecked yet again, this time somewhere off the Croatian coast. Marooned and desperate for more ships, he had no qualms about swapping the legendary great-sword Excalibur for more vessels and managed to make it to the mainland with only a handful of men. But he then faced a treacherous land-route back across central Europe. His heart must have sunk as he was captured near Vienna by his old friend Leopold of Austria, whom he had so humiliated at Acre. Despite the papal injunction that no crusader should be held captive, Leopold, who had also supported the deposed ruler of Cyprus, had no qualms in handing Richard over to the Holy Roman Emperor Henry VI, who promptly imprisoned him in Castle Durstein – 'the archetypal wicked baron's fortress' – high above the Danube. For their nefarious deed, both Leopold and Henry VI were promptly excommunicated by Pope Celestine III.

But Richard was not to be subdued. An illicit affair with his captor's daughter prompted the humiliated Emperor into releasing a starved lion into Richard's cell. Forewarned of this Machiavellian plot, his lover had provided Richard with 40 silk handkerchiefs. With these he bound his arm before thrusting it to the hilt into the beast's jaws and down its throat. He pulled its heart from its chest and, with it still beating, strode to the Great Hall, where he threw it on the table before his host. The silence was only broken by Richard eating it there and then, seasoned with salt. 'The Lionheart' in more ways than one. He then refused to show any deference to his imperial host, famously declaring, *'I am born of a rank which recognises no superior but God.'*

Thereafter, the legend says that it was the love and sense of duty of his own troubadour, Blondel, which facilitated his final escape, thereby converting Richard from imprisoned king to fairytale hero. In a quest which took him to the walls of almost every castle in Germany, Blondel sat outside their Gothic windows and sang the first line of a ballad he had composed with Richard in earlier times. He then waited until, eventually, he heard it answered by the strong voice of the lion-hearted King rising from the dungeons. Only Richard would have known the second line: he had found his master. Thereafter, the negotiations for his ransom could begin, negotiations which ended with his mother raising a staggering 150,000 Marks (very approximately £15m) in ransom monies.

And despite both his own brother John and King Philip

of France trying to pay Henry to *keep* Richard in prison, after 14 months, on the 4th February 1194 Richard was freed. On being tipped-off that Richard had finally escaped from his Continental incarceration one treacherous English knight promptly died of fright. When the King of France sent John the urgent and coded message, 'Look to yourself; The devil is loose', there must have been some anxious moments back in England. Despite the rumours, some still refused to believe he would ever return.

But by March he had once more returned to an anxious, weary and impoverished England. That the English had been prepared to finance the ransom of their French-speaking King despite his long absence speaks volumes to his stature and popularity. Indeed, it is testament to the importance of a successful foreign policy for political leaders who seek to impose unpopular strictures at home.

For those rebels who had backed the scheming John, there was little cheer at his homecoming. Famously, of course, it was at Nottingham where King Richard's pageant of celebration reached its denouement. For those traitors holed up in that great castle with their infamous sheriff, it must have been an uneasy spectacle to watch the executioner's scaffolds being built around their walls for their own personal despatch. When King Richard finally swept into the castle in person with the challenge, *'Well, am I here?'* the state of their breeches can only be imagined.

That the evil Sheriff of Nottingham got his comeuppance and that the elusive outlaw Robin Hood was pardoned is still so familiar to our children 800 years later that it might as well be true. It is a mark of the man, Richard, that he forgave his young brother with the words, *'You are only a child.'* Of course, that child went on to become Bad King John on Richard's death. However, that Richard has gone down in history as 'Lionheart' and his brother as 'Soft sword' and 'Lack land' is perhaps a telling exception to the rule that history is the history of the survivor.

A man of action to the end, Richard left England having

spent a total of only six months within these shores. As Sellar and Yeatman once again so irreverently put it, 'Whenever he returned to England he always set out again immediately for the Mediterranean and was therefore known as *Richard Gare de Lyon*.' That his popularity endured such apparent neglect of his own land illustrates the mystique of the man. No sooner had he restored order to England, he headed to France to safeguard his lands there and immediately set about building the epitome of a medieval castle at Castel Gaillard. Indeed, the architecture and scale of this château, the remains of which still survive perched above the Seine, 40 miles north of Paris, were a wonder of the time and incorporated designs not seen in other medieval castles for another 100 years. A masterpiece of military architecture, the design is attributed to Richard himself who did not retain an architect. And from that impregnable base, he then proceeded to defeated the French in their own backyard throughout 1198. Giving the French a bloody-nose has always been a popular move back home.

A modern photograph of the Castel Gaillard ruins

But of course, it would be unbefitting the life of a *true* hero to have such a fairytale ending. And on the 26th March 1199, whilst successfully besieging Château Chalus Chabrol, he was hit by a crossbow bolt to the shoulder which soon turned gangrenous. Having swiftly taken the castle, the English located the young French sniper and threw him before their dying King. In the interview, the courageous boy explained that Richard had been responsible for the death of his father and his two brothers. Whether it was his respect for the boy's courage or an attempt at a last-minute death-bed act of Christian mercy, with the words, *'Live on and by my bounty behold the light of day,'* he sent the boy away with his life and 100 shillings. A humble, forgiving yet noble gesture: the final act of a torrid life. 'The Lion by the Ant was slain.' Within 10 days, Richard died in the arms of his one true love, his mother, Eleanor of Aquitaine.

His heart was buried in Rouen Cathedral where it still remains, preserved and embalmed in frankincense; sufficiently intact that it was still able to be forensically examined as recently as 2012, some 800 years after its last beat.

Bizarrely, despite the fact that he was married, that he left an illegitimate son, Philip of Cognac, and that he reputedly took several mistresses when 'on campaign', there have been attempts over the centuries to hijack Richard's reputation for being a 'man's man' and to over-interpret his reluctance to marry. He is often described as being fine and long-limbed of figure and possessing striking strawberry-blond hair. And, it is true that, as a bachelor, the role of 'queen' at his Coronation was played by his mother, Eleanor. But when you consider that he spent almost every day of his 10-year reign either at war, imprisoned, escaping or being ship-wrecked, and mostly thousands of miles from his homeland, I suppose it may just be the case that he simply found it difficult to meet girls. Certainly he lived a paradoxical life. That he meted out vicious punishment to his enemies with apparent relish is beyond doubt. But he had a gentler side too. After a good meal, he promptly knighted his cook. And before his death, he granted a life-pension to his former wet-nurse. But whatever the truth of his sexuality, for a hero as monumental as Richard, being celebrated as a gay icon is probably no big deal. It is simply another string to his bow.

He has been described by the eminent Sir Steven Runciman as 'a bad son, a bad husband and a bad king'.* Yet despite even those wholly disparaging criticisms, that same historian has no choice but to at least grant that he was 'a gallant and splendid soldier'. And for all of his many failings, 'The glory that he sought was that of victory rather than conquest.' It was neither the prizes nor the taking part that Richard wanted: it was simply the winning.

'If heroism be confined to brutal and ferocious valour, Richard will stand high among the heroes of the age', wrote Edward Gibbon in *The Decline and Fall of the Roman Empire* in 1776. Richard still stands today, as a colossus between the two Houses of Parliament, astride his charger and adorned by chain mail, sword aloft and the cross of St George aflutter. King, Knight, Legend and Hero.

> Now, by this light, were I to get again,
> Madam, I would not wish a better father:
> Some sins do bear their privilege on earth,
> And so doth yours: your fault was not your folly.
> Needs must you lay your heart at his dispose,
> Subjected tribute to commanding Love,
> Against whose fury and unmatchéd force
> The aweless lion could not wage the fight,
> Nor keep his princely heart from Richard's hand.
> He that perforce robs lions of their hearts,
> May easily win a woman's. Aye, my mother,
> With all my heart, I thank thee for my father.**

Shakespeare was still praising the man and the legend, some 400 years after Richard's death.

---

* This and the following two quotations come from Runciman's book *A History of the Crusades*, 1954.

** Speech by Philip the Bastard to his mother, Lady Faulconbridge, about his father, Richard I: William Shakespeare, *King John*, Act I, Scene 1.

RICHARD I: HERO PROFILE

Beat the French

Humiliated the Austrians

Conquered Cyprus

Took his wife on crusade for their honeymoon

Escaped from a German castle

Fought a path to Jerusalem

Made peace with the Muslims

Killed a lion with his hands

Cut an iron bar in two with his great sword

'The Bard' wrote a stanza praising him in his play, King John

Forgave his killer

Imprisoned the Sheriff of Nottingham

Freed Robin Hood

Gave England St George and 'three lions'

Sir William Wallace
Braveheart

WARRIOR, MAN OF principle, statesman and legend: the legacy of William Wallace spans over 700 years. He remains the most heroic Scot who has ever lived, as famous and relevant now as he ever was.

A minor noble who took up the cause of the common man, Wallace became the commander-in-chief of the Scots army and was elected the Guardian of Scotland. By standing up to the military superiority of Edward I's empire-building Plantagenet England, he kept Scotland independent from the marauding English for the last 15 years of his life and is ultimately responsible for preserving full Scottish independence until the Act of Union 400 years later.

'He was a tall man with the body of a giant, cheerful

in appearance with agreeable features, broad-shoul-
dered and big boned, with belly in proportion and
lengthy flanks, pleasing in appearance but with a wild
look… a most spirited fighting man with all his limbs
very strong and firm.'
(From the 14th century *Scotichronicon*.)

Whatever his true stature, we know that his broadsword
measured 5 ft 4 inches itself. It would have taken someone
of immense strength and size to effectively wield such a
weapon. One can see how the legend grew.

In the end, having narrowly escaped death on several
occasions, he was hanged several times almost to the point
of death, drawn and quartered in the most barbaric of
executions. But this grotesque end only served to fuel the
legend and inflame Scottish nationalism until the present
day. At a time when most of the Scottish aristocracy could
readily be bought by English silver, Wallace could never
be bribed. He was the very epitome of a true Scot, who
had burning within him 'The spirit of a race as stern and
resolute as has ever been bred among men'.*

Historical context

As with so many medieval figures, his origins are shrouded
in mystery. Born in approximately 1272, a younger son of
minor Scottish nobility, he was educated by an uncle-priest
at Cambuskenneth Abbey where he studied the classics. It
is said that it was there that he learned the Latin phrase
which fortified his entire existence: *'No gift is like to liber-
tie; then never live in slaverie.'*

To understand Wallace and appreciate his determined
and desperate heroism, one needs a little historical context.

* Winston Churchill: *A History of the English Speaking Peoples*,
Vol. 1.

Within two years of Wallace's birth, King Henry III of England died and was succeeded by his son, Edward I 'Longshanks', later given the sobriquet 'Hammer of the Scots' and the man destined to be Wallace's arch-rival. Then the peaceful and prosperous reign of Alexander III of Scotland came to a premature end on the 19th March 1286, when Alexander fell from his horse and down a cliff face during a storm. His two sons having recently predeceased their father, the country was plunged into a power vacuum. The only remaining direct heir to the Scottish royal line had been Alexander's three-year-old granddaughter, Margaret, the 'Maid of Norway'.

Edward I had agreed with the King of Norway that the 'Maid' would be betrothed to his own five-year-old son, Edward, Prince of Wales (later Edward II). Had she been, English influence in Scotland would have been assured through the legitimate union between the two sovereign families. But she perished in a shipwreck off the Orkney coast en route to Scotland in 1290, by then aged just six years old; and with her perished the Royal House of Dunkeld which had reigned in Scotland for the previous 250 years.

Consequently, Edward's carefully crafted diplomacy designed to secure legitimate influence in Scotland was frustrated. The 'guardianship' he had exercised over Scotland as an interim measure lost its mandate and rival Scottish grandees, from such families as Bruce and Balliol, began manoeuvring for power. To avoid civil war and as a legitimate arbiter between the rival factions, Edward I of England was invited to adjudicate between the disparate claims.

Whilst he deliberated between the 15 contenders, he forced a number of concessions from the Scots, adopted the mantle of overlord of Scotland, directed that whoever he chose would be subservient to his own kinship and placed constables in key Scottish castles, ostensibly to 'keep the peace'. Indeed, all Scots were ordered to pay homage to him by July 1291.

However, although Wallace's own grandfather, Sir Reginald de Crauford, was the sheriff responsible for administering the homages of allegiance in Ayr, Sir Reginald noticed that his own family's names did not appear on the roll. Wallace's father had refused to 'bend the knee.'

By this defiant act, William Wallace's father, Sir Malcolm, had sealed the fate of his own family and specifically that of his middle son, William. Sending his wife and family, including young William to Dundee, Sir Malcolm Wallace fled north to Lennox where, late in 1291, he was hunted down and murdered by an English knight at Loudoun Hill because of his refusal to bow to English supremacy.

*14th-century French illustration of John Balliol
before Edward I*

By the time John Balliol had been adjudicated king of Scotland by Edward I over all other claimants and been enthroned on the Stone of Scone on St Andrew's Day 1292, Edward had established a firm foothold in Scotland and was clearly the new King John's feudal overlord, having demanded he swear allegiance to him as his Lord

Paramount on Boxing Day 1292: symbolically, a swearing-in ceremony conducted on English soil at Newcastle. As a further calculated insult to the Scots and as an inadvertent warning of what was in store, Edward had the Great Seal of Scotland smashed to pieces and sent down to Westminster.

Over the next three years, Edward proceeded to make the new King John's life as difficult as possible. By political double-dealing, he encouraged Norway to reclaim the Western Isles, gave continued hope to several of the unsuccessful claimants for the Crown and heard appeals from King John's own pronouncements in English courts; the upshot of which was a divided Scotland and a thoroughly undermined and weak King John, now nicknamed 'Toon Tabard' or 'empty coat' for his alleged spinelessness. King John may well have been a puppet to the English King, but in reality he had little choice. And in fairness to John, when in September 1294 Edward demanded Scottish troops to assist him in prosecuting his English war against France, even King John could not bear the humiliation and refused, instead forging a treaty with King Philip IV of France himself. This had the calculated effect of bringing the grievances between the Scottish and English crowns to a head.

In retaliation for his defiance, in October 1295, all King John's English estates were seized. A fleet of English warships was sent up the East coast to Newcastle. By March 1296, massed forces of English and Scottish militia were facing each other across the border. Notably absent from the Scottish side of the line were the Earls of Carrick, Angus and Dundee who had chosen to side with the English.

After months of skirmishes, political chicanery and looting by both sides, on the 30th March 1296, Edward himself rode up to Berwick's town gates with an army of 35,000 men, invited their unconditional surrender and was jeered and insulted for his offer. But on this occasion, the Scottish bark was worse than its bite and Edward's army easily breached their defences, overran the town and in torching it to the ground committed one of the worst massacres ever recorded on British soil. Up to 20,000 Scottish souls perished over the following three days in calculated revenge for their temerity and specifically to avenge the death of Edward's cousin, Richard of Cornwall, whose brain had been pierced by an arrow entering through the eye-slit of his helmet during the attack.

Retaliation followed. King John formally renounced his allegiance to the English King. Scottish troops raided across the border into Northumberland. English garrisons in Scottish castles were harassed and the Scots took Dunbar Castle. Using this pretext, the English marched into Scotland on the 27th April 1296 and the Scottish army was either routed or fled at the ignominious battle of Dunbar. One hundred and thirty of Scotland's most important and loyal knights were captured, including its commander-in-chief, John Comyn Earl of Buchan. Dunbar, Roxborough, Jedburgh and Edinburgh castles fell and many others surrendered over the spring and early summer. In any event, by July 1296 King John had no realistic choice but to surrender his crown, abdicate and plead for forgiveness.

This he did by publicly admitting his errors, donning a plain white robe and formally abdicating at the feet of Edward at Montrose on 10th July 1296. King John's and Scotland's shame was complete. After a three-year incarceration in the Tower of London, John, former King of Scotland, was exiled to France where he died some 14 years later, blind, broken and forgotten. A pitiful character in a humiliating Scottish chapter. Humiliating because, despite the propaganda painting Scotland in the 13th century as a primitive nation living at the very edge of civilisation, in fact it was a proud and cultured nation, rich in architecture and learning, and adorned with many cathedrals and abbeys, palaces and castles and one which had just enjoyed 37 years of peace and reasonable prosperity under Alexander III.

With King John consigned to history, Edward had himself crowned King of Scotland at Scone on the 'stone of destiny' before transporting that sacred symbol of Scottishness down to Westminster Abbey, where it remained for 700 years until, on the 15th November 1996, it finally returned to Scotland. In August 1296, some 2,000 Scottish nobles signed up to English supremacy in the infamous document known as the 'Ragman Roll'. The Wallace name was once again notable by its absence.

Edward left English garrisons in several key Scottish castles and was now poised to annex Scotland as he had Wales just a few years earlier. With his work in Scotland all but accomplished, he left for London, his contempt for the Scots he was leaving behind evident from his parting comment, 'He who rids himself of shit does a good job.' Hardly diplomatic.

Replica of the Stone of Scone at Scone Palace, Perth

The early years

It had been in these miserable and divided times that William Wallace's own father, Sir Malcolm had been killed by an English knight in a skirmish back in 1291.

Perhaps it was that which catalysed the resentment and defiance which was to characterise Wallace's life hereinafter, for, with his father's loss still raw in his heart, he was drawn into a confrontation which was to change the course of his life irrevocably. In December of that same year, a man named Selby, son of the English constable of Dundee castle, insulted and taunted Wallace over the very recent murder of his father. Understandably unable to contain his anger and resentment, Wallace instinctively stabbed Selby clean through the heart for his English arrogance. As Wallace made his escape, the die of his life had been cast: he was to remain an outlaw in the eyes of the English forever thereafter.

Having escaped, allegedly by disguising himself as an elderly woman spinning at the wheel, he then took to his heels, ultimately reaching an uncle at Ellerslie by February 1292. He had spent two months on the run with an ever-increasing bounty on his head. Whilst supposedly lying low at Riccarton near Kilmarnock, on the 23rd April 1292, he was found fishing on the River Irvine when he was approached by a garrison of English soldiers. When they demanded his catch, Wallace suggested a halfway split, but he was attacked for his insolence. In self-defence, he struck one with his fishing pole, seized another's sword and decapitated him, before maiming two others and causing the rest to flee.

Aged 20, he was a wanted man and one who faced certain death if caught. He fled on to the Leglen Woods: desperate, homeless and hunted. He existed as a vagrant. But being on the run was not something Wallace could tolerate indefinitely. Visiting the market town of Ayr, he encountered a burly English street entertainer who, for the price of one 'groat', challenged all comers to hit him as hard as they liked with a wooden pole. This temptation was too much for Wallace to resist: he gave him three groats and struck him with such force that he broke the Englishman's back. In the ensuing melée with the

English garrison, Wallace once more fled to the woods. This defiant risk-taking continued, but his luck could not hold indefinitely. Witnessing one of his kinsman's servants being bullied by an English steward, Wallace could not resist intervening. As the steward lunged at him with his hunting staff, Wallace grabbed him and stabbed him to death with his dirk. As the garrison converged upon him, despite putting up herculean resistance, he was overwhelmed and, not before time perhaps, thrown in gaol. Injured, captured, helpless and facing trial and inevitable execution, he succumbed to a fever and fell into a coma. But in an almost miraculous turn of events, his unconscious body was found by the gaoler, who presumed that he had died. He was thrown from the city walls onto the communal midden.

It is here that almost unbelievable chance plays its hand and the seed of the legend was planted. His former nursemaid, hearing of his death, sought and was granted permission to recover the body for a decent burial. Taking him to a safe house and detecting some weak signs of life, she slowly nursed him back to health, albeit keeping up the pretence that he had died. But the truth slowly seeped out.

The rumours surrounding Wallace's miraculous recovery came to the attention of the famous soothsayer, Sir Thomas Rymour who penned his prophetic verse about Wallace and his beloved Scotland:

> 'For sooth, ere he decease,
> Shall many thousands in the field make end,
> From Scotland he shall forth the Southron send,
> And Scotland thrice he shall bring to peace.
> So good of hand again shall ne'er be kenned.'

It would seem that his early defiance of the English occupation and his reckless resistance to it as epitomised by 'Thomas the Rhymer' started the ball of legend rolling. It certainly provided Wallace with a destiny, as foretold by the same man who had prophesied the death of King Alexander III. And by that royal association, it made both Scots and English alike sit up and take notice. But it takes more than a couple of pig-headed skirmishes and a poem to create a legend.

Certainly, whatever Wallace's virtues, remaining inconspicuous was not amongst them. Deciding to walk to Riccarton after his recovery to present himself to his uncle, Sir Richard Wallace, he was challenged by three English mounted soldiers on the road. The interrogation went badly and as they went to arrest him, Wallace produced his sword and dispatched the men before making off with their three horses, some weapons and a sack of food. The cat was now well and truly out of the bag.

His inspirational 'resurrection', combined with his daring and defiant resistance, caused a small trickle of friends, kinsmen and desperadoes to support and follow him: perhaps out of loyalty, perhaps in the desperate hope that he could act as a rallying figure for their own ideals; perhaps as a last resort to try and save their own skins or change their own fortunes. So, starting as a small-time outlaw and fighting for his life, he began looting and attacking any English garrison which came to his notice. As the number of his followers grew, so did his audacity. The English occupiers were about to discover a form of resistance they were at a loss to know how to tackle. In effect, he had started a campaign of guerrilla warfare 650 years before such an expression was coined.

In July 1296, as Scotland's humiliation reached its zenith, Wallace got wind of intelligence that Fenwick, the English knight responsible for murdering his father five years earlier, was commanding a convoy of bullion being transferred between the two English garrison strongholds, Lanark and Ayr. Provided with the date, route and size of the convoy, Wallace planned an ambush. Selecting the narrowing track running through a gorge at Loudoun Hill, his band of just 50 rebels fabricated a landslide to narrow the path still further. As the convoy slowed at the obstacle, Wallace attacked, initially at the front of the column to prevent its escape and then in its midst. Targeting the horses of the mounted knights and cavalry, his men thrust their swords and spears into their unprotected underbellies, felling them or disabling them and causing their riders to be dismounted. Catching sight of Fenwick himself, Wallace slashed his Claymore across the knight's horse's girth and stirrup leathers, dismounting him before he was dispatched by Wallace's cousin, Robert Boyd. Fenwick was one of 100 English soldiers killed in the attack. Only 80 survivors escaped, leaving Wallace with 200 packhorses laden with treasure and provisions. He also won huge quantities of armour, weaponry and a few of the surviving cavalry horses. Wallace's troop had lost three men, but they had won a morale-boosting victory and one which had shattered the sense of English invincibility.

A spree of similarly opportunistic pillages followed, enthusiastically executed by his ever-growing band of exiles, outlaws and malcontents. This gang of rough men, seeking him out in the wilds of Dunbartonshire, were responsible for looting Sir Henry de Percy's baggage train, which drove this English knight into seeking a truce with this 'awful chieftain'. But, after initially accepting a truce for the sake of his uncle, Sir Reginald de Crauford (who had miraculously managed to hold onto his position as sheriff of Ayr), Wallace found he was simply not prepared or able to abide by the English terms. Indeed, he slighted the truce in blatant form, attacking Sir Henry de Percy's own baggage train for a second time, looting it and leaving five more dead English soldiers.

A litany of skirmishes and raids followed: Gargunnock Peel tower, Methven Wood, then Kinclaven castle, which was plundered, purged of every soldier and set ablaze. A rising tally of English knights was being notched on Wallace's broadsword and the price on his head rose steadily.

In the ensuing reprisals, the English launched a whole-sale offensive, outnumbering Wallace ten to one. Despite inflicting casualties on the English by luring them into the woods, eventually Wallace had to melt away into the forests. But he was tracked down to a rocky craig which he resolved to defend by confronting the early arrivals rather than awaiting the full English force. He slaughtered the advance party before escaping to Elcho Park with just 43 men left in his band. But until Wallace was captured, the English were not minded to give up. Sir John Butler continued to hound them until they had scattered, leaving Wallace alone and injured by an arrow wound to the neck. In such a desperate state he was found by Butler who, on the very brink of arresting him, was attacked by Wallace who inflicted a gash to his thigh, slit his throat, stole his horse and, yet again, fled for his life.

He rode the horse for 15 miles to exhaustion, leaving it where it fell before escaping across the icy waters of the River Forth to the south bank at Cambuskenneth, near Stirling. Sheltered by a family who took him in, provisioned him and hid him, it was rumoured he had perished once again, this time in the river: a rumour he was happy to encourage. But Wallace could not play dead for long. Gathering together his most trusted men, he made for the relative safety of Dundaff and Gilbank before dispatching his inner circle to spread word of his survival and to try and drum up support once more.

By now it was the Christmas of 1296. And despite the privations which must have beset him, Wallace was mortal flesh. And, like so many inspirational figures, he had something of a reputation for the ladies. Wallace's weakness at this time was a young woman he had met whilst attending church in Lanark.

Marion Bradfute was a beautiful eighteen-year-old heiress, but a catch the Sheriff of Lanark, Sir William Heselrig, had his own eye on as a match for his son John.

But Wallace would secretly visit her regardless, and in due course won her.

However, this was not to be an enduring relationship, because Wallace never allowed self-interest to divert him from his relentless resistance to English occupation. Whether it was simply out of military necessity or as vengeance for the multitude of wrongs he perceived had been meted out by these imposters, Wallace's actions were like a cold sword through the hearts of the English nobility. Sir Robert de Clifford, a nephew of Sir Henry de Percy, was killed for insulting Wallace and his companions having jealously cut off their horses' tails. In the ensuing hue and cry, Sir Hugh de Morland also fell to the Wallace sword. These successes swelled Wallace's numbers, with men of importance gathering under his banner: Sir John Graham joined him and his backing gave Wallace the confidence to secure or lay waste to a few castles. Then in the Spring of 1297, he found time to return to Lanark where he hastily married Marion in a secret ceremony.

Whatever happiness they found was short-lived. In May 1297 the Sheriff of Lanark engineered an ambush of which Wallace himself would have been proud. He got an English soldier to confront Wallace in town. As Wallace started to rise to the taunts, more and more soldiers arrived. Wallace could see what was happening and tried to leave the town, noticing that English soldiers were poorly disguised as locals and waiting for the trap to be sprung. Escaping down a narrow side street, he was able to flee, whilst fighting a rearguard action. The narrowness of the streets prevented the soldiers from confronting him in numbers. And it allowed Wallace enough time to reach the only safe house he had, that of Marion Bradfute at the foot of the High Street. Having taken very temporary refuge, he and his small retinue fled from the back garden, over the town walls and out to their hide-out in the Cartland Crags. But despite his escape and the 50 or so English soldiers they had left dead or injured in their wake, it was to be a pyrrhic victory for Wallace. For after Sir John Heselrig had tired of Marion's delaying tactics, he ordered his men to kick in her door. Seeing that his prey had fled, in a rage he had Marion murdered on the spot and then torched the family house.

The grief and fury with which Wallace reacted to this news must have been terrible to witness. The English invader had now murdered both his father and his wife. Honour and bitter personal vengeance dictated that Heselrig was going to pay for his crimes, and soon. Returning to Lanark that night, he and his small band of men infiltrated their way into the town in small groups. Having met at a pre-arranged location, they then stormed Sir William Heslerig's castle without any warning. Wallace made straight for the Sheriff's bed-chamber where he summarily decapitated him in his bed before kicking his head down the castle stairs. His son sought to defend the house, but had his sword arm amputated and was disembowelled for his efforts. The castle was set ablaze and Heselrig's entire garrison of 240 soldiers were executed. However, it says something of the man that, despite what must have been an uncontrollable anger, he spared all the women, children and priests from the sword, forcibly evicting them from the town instead. Whatever slim hope there might have been for a political resolution between Wallace and the English had now vanished altogether. A state of all-out confrontation ending in total defeat for one side was now inevitable.

Despite their vast superiority in numbers, resources and wealth, a sense of considerable unease ran through the English invaders as Wallace's reputation spread amongst the Scots. When Wallace let it be known that he intended to liberate the sacred site of Scone from its occupation by the hated English Justiciar of Scotland, William Ormesby, such was the state of trepidation that Ormesby and his household simply fled, leaving a stash of booty behind them.

Engraving of William Wallace, circa 1700

Guardian

It was Wallace's uncompromising and defiant actions such as these which galvanised an otherwise oppressed and insulted people. Swelling his troop from 50 to 3,000 men, Wallace began to attract more men with real military stature. Gilbert de Grimsby, a Scot by birth and a distinguished commander of Edward's Flanders campaign, defected from the English army. The Bishop of Glasgow encouraged Wallace and gave his cause credibility. The Bishop's own brother-in-law, Sir William Douglas, had also by now joined the rebels. The church were broadly sympathetic to Wallace, being an educated man of faith; but perhaps more pragmatically, they were antipathetic towards Edward, knowing full well his plan to replace their 'kirk' with his English priests.

But Wallace's increasingly irresistible force was up against the immovable object of Edward I's desire to subjugate Scotland. As he saw it, Wallace had precipitated a flagrant rebellion in Scotland, which could not be tolerated. To deal with Sir William Douglas's defection, Edward seized all of his English estates and sent Robert Bruce, the Second Earl of Carrick, to arrest him. However, Bruce himself, no doubt sensing a change in the political tide, promptly changed sides and joined with Douglas in an orgy of revenge attacks against the English in Ayrshire. Alarmed by their loss of control, Edward appointed an English judge to hold a bogus court hearing as to the state of affairs. Summoning the leading Ayrshire landowners to 'The Barns of Ayr' for a 'conference', Edward sought to beguile his foes. But it was a sham, a trick, a trap. For on their arrival on the 18th June 1297, 360 Scottish landowners were herded into a barn and all 360 of them were hung. It was a despicable crime and one which still resonates.

Unsurprisingly, Wallace and the people of Ayr were beside themselves with outrage. The judge and soldiers who had carried out this atrocity were tracked down, barricaded into the same barns and burned alive. In Ayrshire alone that night, 5,000 English died. These extreme acts of violence on both sides had served to achieve that which, only weeks earlier, had seemed impossible: a Scotland in an almost total state of rebellion.

But despite the stakes having been raised yet again, Edward I insisted on the uncompromising prosecution of his campaign into Scotland. He was not nicknamed the 'Hammer of the Scots' for nothing. This time there was to be no second chances: he dispatched Percy and Clifford with 40,000 soldiers to track down the rebels, imprison them and stamp out the rebellion. But whilst this quickly resulted in a truce between many Scottish nobles and the English by 7th July and led to the incarceration of Douglas and his brother the Bishop of Glasgow, Wallace himself remained at large, persistently attacking the English lines of supply before evaporating into the woods. Whilst it would have been open to Wallace, even at this point, to seek to negotiate terms, no doubt securing position and wealth for himself, he chose to fight for what he believed to be right: Scottish freedom and independence. Perhaps, bearing in mind his own personal tragedies, he perceived he had no moral alternative.

Despite the persistent tendency of the Scottish nobility to turn-coat at the first whiff of a change in fortune, by late summer 1297 Wallace had organised the rebel army once again and lifted its morale to such a height that they were able capture the city of Perth, putting 2,000 Englishmen to the sword. Next was Dunottar Castle, instilling such fear in the English occupants that they chose to hurl themselves from the battlements and cliffs rather than face the wrath of their Scottish attackers. Wallace moved all the way to Aberdeen, there surprising an armada of 100 English ships which he looted and burned before causing the English sheriff of Aberdeen to seize the castle in the name of the Scottish king, King John. Wallace's momentum drove him across the Grampians to the Spey, then back again to the siege of Dundee where he freed the town. By August, the bulk of the lands north of the Forth and the Clyde were back under Scottish control. Indeed, The English treasurer of Scotland, Hugh Cressingham, was forced to write to Edward I conceding that:

'by far the greater part of your counties of the realm of Scotland are still unprovided with keepers... so that no county is in proper order, except Berwick and Roxburgh, and this only lately.'

But Dundee and Stirling castles still held out, heavily defended by the increasingly desperate English occupiers. And leaving a token force to maintain the siege in Dundee, Wallace directed his forces to regroup and march for Stirling. Things were about to get even tougher.

By mid-August, the English had a total of nearly 60,000 foot soldiers and a heavy cavalry of well over 1,000 horse converging on Stirling to reinforce the hard-pressed garrison there and to try and lift the siege at Dundee. Indeed, so confident was Edward of his superiority, that on the 22nd he left for Flanders, not to return to England for over six months.

On 6th September 1297, Wallace watched the advance of the English army from his vantage point on the Ochil Hills, overlooking the River Forth and the rocky crag upon which sat Stirling castle. Behind him he had a maximum of 16,000 men and a small armed cavalry. But he had the high ground and he had followers of unquenchable fighting spirit, burning with the injustice of the past few years and its countless atrocities. In contrast, the English were camped on the valley floor, facing the narrow wooden bridge which afforded the only close point to cross the river. Additionally, for once it was not the Scots in disarray but the English. It would seem they had been unsettled by Wallace's reply to their recent invitation to surrender:

'Let them come up when they like, and they will find us ready to meet them even to their beards.'

This graphic challenge must have caused the hairs on the backs of their English necks to stand on end; in their agitation, despite being advised to avoid the bridge and instead ford the river a short distance to the East, the bickering and unsettled command of Cressingham and de Warenne decided to simply take the enemy head-on by crossing the bridge and attacking them up hill.

It was now that Wallace really demonstrated his calm and experience as a commander of fighting men. He had to strike a balance between allowing a sufficient contingent of the English army to cross the bridge so that they were committed, and maintaining a sufficient numerical advantage as to make a successful confrontation realistic. At 11.00 am, from the summit of Abbey Craig, Wallace gave the signal to attack with a single blast of his horn. But this was no undisciplined rebel horde. As the main body of the infantry ran at the English to shouts of 'On them! On them!' a second detachment headed directly to the bridgehead, to block any chance of retreat or rein-forcement and thereby close the trap. And it worked. As the rebels took control of the North side of the bridge, the English panicked. Some tried to retreat back across the bridge whilst others were still advancing and were unable to stop those behind them doing likewise. The upshot was a stampede in which soldiers, knights and armoured horses fell, jumped or were knocked into the river to their deaths, or were trampled underfoot. The main body of the English force was not faring much better. Caught off-guard by the speed and ferocity of the Scottish attack, they were cut down or driven backwards, into the dead end of the loop in the river and its marshy flood plain. Despite a brave cavalry charge by the English, the colours of the King and the Earl of Surrey were both lost and the bridge fell under the control of the Scots, cutting off the retreat for those committed to the north bank.

In the panic the English commanders ordered the bridge be destroyed, thereby preventing any Scottish attack across the Forth. But it had the effect of sacrificing virtually every English soldier unable to swim for his life from the north side. With all the Welsh archers having been committed in the vanguard, they were exterminated and unable to provide any arrow cover for the remainder of the English forces. After an hour of butchery by the Scots, almost the entire English advance party of 5,000 soldiers, 100 cavalry and 300 archers had been wiped out. John de Warenne had been thoroughly humiliated and turned on his heel, barely stopping before he reached the safety of the English border. By the time he received the message from Edward I's son, the Prince of Wales, that he was to stay in Scotland until the rebellion was quashed, Warenne was already back in York and heading south.

One of the many dead left behind was Hugh Cressing-ham, the hated English Treasurer of Scotland whose body, upon its discovery, was flayed of its skin and used to make a baldric for Wallace's own sword. The defeat of the English at the momentous battle of Stirling Bridge was, in retrospect, the zenith of Wallace's military career and one for which, as the new Commander-in-Chief of the Scottish army, he was knighted in the name of King John. He was promptly elected the Guardian of Scotland by his peers. This was a remarkable vote of confidence in a man who did not hail from the normal ruling class and who was still regarded with suspicion by much of the Scottish nobility. Almost inevitably, Stirling quickly capitulated to the Scots, rapidly followed by Dundee. Indeed, despite determined resistance from the last few surviving garrisons, by the end of October 1297, English control in Scotland was virtually non-existent. However, because of the scorched earth policy adopted by the retreating English, they had left the Scots with the problem of a regional food shortage. To alleviate the impending crisis, Wallace embarked on a campaign of cross-border raiding and on the 18th October he marched the Scottish army into England across the Tweed. After two months of deliberate and sustained plundering, he re-crossed the border, taking with him as many English provision as his army could carry, drag or consume.

These early Scottish wars of independence marked a turning point, a departure from the traditional warfare. Chivalric display and set-piece battle was replaced by tactical attack, skirmish and ambush using the natural landscape and the element of surprise to counteract numerical inequality. It is really as that opportunistic leader and rebel commander that Wallace excelled and upon which his reputation was built. Out of necessity, he had invented 'guerrilla warfare': a lasting and significant legacy, if not a particularly splendid or happy one.

After news of this audacious Scottish cross-border *chevauchee* reached Edward in April 1298, a second wholesale invasion of Scotland was mounted. But Wallace was not to be intimidated and he toyed with Edward, shadowing his army and luring it deeper into Scotland whilst all the while harassing its lines of supply, hoping thereby to starve and extend it into an enforced retreat. It was a tactic which bore results and which, had he been allowed to continue, could have been decisive. Indeed, such was the state of starvation and exhaustion in the English ranks that the infantry mutinied, only to be brought to order by their own cavalry. Edward was increasingly desperate to engage the Scots but he had to wait for three hungry months before the opportunity arose. As his army headed to Edinburgh, he heard that Wallace was camped near Falkirk and, desperate to engage, he prepared for imminent battle and diverted to face the Scots. Wallace was probably caught slightly unprepared, but again was undaunted. He selected a good defensive site, on rising ground and fronted by a stream and marshy ground to make life hard for the English heavy cavalry. He then formed his infantry spear-men into four circles or 'schiltrons': 2,000 men strong and surrounded by a palisade of sharpened stakes driven into the soft ground and bound together with heavy ropes. This was the first time such a device was ever used in the British Isles and one which must be attributed to Wallace. Before the inevitable onslaught, Wallace demonstrated his humour and leadership, encouraging his own men with:

'I have brought you to the ring. Now dance the best you can.'

The English heavy cavalry repeatedly charged this 'impenetrable hedge' of the Scottish schiltron from all sides, and 111 of their horses and dozens of their knights perished upon their spikes. Indeed, such was the resilience of the Scottish infantrymen and so great the losses amongst the English cavalry, that Edward was forced to change tack. It was at this point he deployed the Lancastrian and Welsh bowmen, who achieved what the cavalry had failed to.

They were able to force openings in the Scottish circles, which the cavalry could then seek to exploit. But still, all need not have been lost. Valiant fighting by the small Scots cavalry lead by such figures as Macduff, Earl of Fife, was still offering enough protection for the schiltrons to regroup and hold. But then, once again, when things started to get rough, the Scottish nobles succumbed to treachery. The unforgivable decision by 'Red' John Commyn and other members of the Scottish nobility to simply withdraw their regiments from the battlefield was crippling to Wallace's position and decisive of the outcome. It left the Scots at a massive numerical disadvantage, exposed and sapped of confidence.

A 19th-century recreation of the Battle of Falkirk

With gaps emerging in the schiltrons and the English cavalry now riding unchecked, the English infantry were sent in to finish off the job. With the exception of Wallace and his immediate staff, there was nobody left to defend them. As the Scottish remnant turned and fled, they were cut down by another contingent of English cavalry which had outflanked them. It became a rout and by the end 10,000 Scots lay dead on the field of battle. Wallace was forced to flee to his familiar sanctuary of the woods where, in more familiar terrain, he could hide, regroup and attack his pursuers in manageable numbers. It was no failing of Wallace that things had disintegrated; but it was a lasting example of the Scottish ability to self-destruct.

Whether it was that Wallace had been slightly caught by surprise, whether it was because of internal jealousies mounting within the Scottish nobility against this upstart commander or whether it was simply superiority of English numbers and longbow firepower, in reality Falkirk was the end for Wallace. Not that he made it easy for the English thereafter. Indeed, in the immediate aftermath of the battle the English army was close to disintegration itself. As Wallace fled the battlefield, he once again tried to starve the English out of Scotland. He razed Stirling and then Perth to prevent the English finding anything to sustain them there. As the English desperately headed for the coast at Ayr and a promised means of escape by sea, the soldiers were reduced to eating their own horses which had themselves just starved to death. But the boats never arrived and Edward was forced to march his starving and mutinous army south, leaving Wallace at large and Scotland cowed but untamed.

Despite these desperate actions, by September 1298, Wallace realised he did not have the backing of the Scottish nobility, if he ever truly had and, after only 300 days as the leader of the Scotland he loved, he resigned his Guardianship in favour of a new triumvirate, headed by Robert the Bruce, the future king of Scotland.

The Legacy

But Wallace had more than one string to his bow. Using his education, his languages and his faith, he reinvented himself as a statesman and ambassador for Scotland, travelling to the continent to press the Scottish cause to the King of France and the Pope in Rome. Indeed, he had some notable success, with a Papal Bull being issued by Pope Boniface VIII to Edward I, stating:

'That from ancient times the Realm of Scotland was not, is not feudally subject to your predecessors, the Kings of England, nor to you.'

This must have made humiliating reading to Edward after all the personal and military capital he had invested in that very cause.

Wallace's indefatigable political manoeuvring behind the scenes contributed to the Scottish resistance which persisted over the next five years until, one by one, every single Scottish noble had been bought with English silver: except Wallace. He refused to swear allegiance to Edward, saying,

'As a freeborn man, so shall I die.'

And, once more, it was to be the enemy within who was to prove his undoing: double-crossed by the self-serving Scottish nobility one last time. At Robroyston, near Glasgow, John de Menteith turned Wallace over to the English as he slept as a guest in his house, for the relatively paltry sum of 30 pieces of silver. It took over two weeks to parade Wallace through the county towns of England as he was dragged south to London. Mocked and insulted through the thronging streets, he was taken to Westminster Hall, his head crowned with the outlaw's garland of oak and tried for treason.

Dignified, courageous and defiant to the end, he answered his charge simply, with irrefutable logic and with the law on his side:

'I could not be a traitor to Edward, For I was never his subject.'

It must have been an uncomfortable silence which followed that unanswerable truth. But, of course, it did nothing to slow his journey to the noose and to an end which must rank amongst the worst imaginable. For sheer bloody cruelty, surely it cannot be outdone. It is perhaps the last mark of respect to the man and the fear and inconvenience he put the English to that it was felt necessary to perpetrate these extremes of torture to his defenceless body. On the 23rd August 1305, hanged several times to the verge of death, castrated, stretched on the wheel, ribs broken and entrails drawn, his heart was pulled from his rib-cage. Miraculously, he lived on defiantly throughout this ordeal until he was finally decapitated and his torment was ended. A plaque remains to commemorate his butchery in Smithfield market, still set into the wall of St Bart's hospital. Incredibly, he was just 33 years of age.

But if Edward thought he could crush the Scottish spirit with this grotesque act of vengeance, he was very wrong. Indeed, in the view of John Prebble, Wallace's horrific execution was a black deed which has, above anything else, 'unified the resolve of the people of Scotland and fortified them.' Ever since.

The beautiful irony of Wallace's death is that it has only been in the centuries which have followed that his significance has truly emerged. Militarily, of course, guerrilla warfare as developed by Wallace was here to stay and still remains. Indeed, many of Wallace's unconventional tactics were adopted by the English and used with devastating effect against the French in the iconic battles of Crécy and Agincourt during the Hundred Years War. The schiltrons he invented at Falkirk were employed successfully against the English again at Bannockburn in 1314. And they formed the basis of those awe-inspiring Scottish squares, deployed with such devastating effect by that great *English* military hero, the Duke of Wellington, at Waterloo nearly 500 years later: the bayonets and muskets replacing the spears and sharpened stakes to repel and decimate the French cavalry.

This is perhaps not the only legacy he has indirectly provided to his English foes. After all, if you think about it, he was a guerrilla leader, hiding in the woods and attacking the baggage trains of the unpopular sheriffs. He was a great fighter, swordsman and leader of men. His true love, Marion, was the daughter of a wealthy gentleman. He had a younger brother, John, and a friend and follower by the name of Edward Little. And his old friend, John Blair, left his monastic life to follow his friend and record his deeds. Who does that remind you of?

He had faced his prosecutors at Westminster Hall with the outlaw's wreath of oak upon his brow. An outlaw. A man of the woods. A freedom fighter. Is it possible that the gruesome derring-do of Wallace, which caused such *worry* to the English at the end of the 13th century has been hi-jacked and transposed, over time, into an Anglo-centric folk-tale, allegedly emerging from the reign of Richard I less than a hundred years earlier? By some political and literary sleight-of-hand, did Wallace ultimately defy his enemy and transcend his time by becoming one of the greatest *English* heroes of all: Robin Hood?

Certainly, the bravery and dignity with which Wallace faced his death inspired many on both sides of the border and won him the many friends he had been denied in his lifetime. Even at the end, he demanded his last Christian rights before he was hung; and the Archbishop of Canterbury defied Edward's orders to grant them to him. But even then there was to be no compromise, no weakness. His final words were:

'I repent of my sins, but it is not of Edward of England that I shall ask pardon.'

Led away to his execution, his final act was to read from his own personal psalm book, mouthing the words to block out the din which surrounded him. His bearing and final actions stand testament to his deeply held Christian beliefs. Indeed, the campaign by some Scottish Catholics to have him canonised continues to this day.

His unwavering belief in personal liberty and the independence of his Scotland is a flame which he alone kept alight in those very dark years and which still burns now. His fight and his legacy was epitomised in the Declaration of Arbroath, sent by a group of Scottish nobles in support of Robert the Bruce 15 years after Wallace's execution. It said this:

'It is in truth not for glory nor riches nor honours that we are fighting, but for freedom – for that alone which no honest man gives up but with life itself... For as long as one hundred of us shall remain alive we shall neverwise consent to submit to the rule of the English.'

The words might have been Wallace's own and for many they remain the legacy of William Wallace, champion of the Scots.

Indeed, ultimately it was Wallace, not Edward, who was the victor. For Edward died near the Scottish border in 1307, his ambitions to subjugate Scotland still unfulfilled. He asked to be buried in a lead casket, and only placed into a golden one once Scotland had been conquered. He still lies in his leaden bed.

Whereas for Sir William, the future was much brighter. The legend of his life was celebrated 170 years after his death in the 15th century epic poem by Blind Harry, *The Wallace*. Whether true or not, in itself it is a testament to the stature of the man. A romantic poem of 11,000 lines, which remained for the next 400 years the most popular printed work in Scottish history, after the Bible. It is a rousing and vivid call to arms to the 'Brave, true ancient Scots' and a celebration of the man to whom it is dedicated.

'First here I honour, in particular, Sir William Wallace, much renowned in war.'

It goes on to eulogise about 'his nobille worthy deeds', specifically, his threefold 'reskew of Scotland' from the English enemy, 'his strength and stalwart hand' and how it was that the Scots 'chose him for chief, chieftain and leader'. It was and still remains a rousing, nationalistic call to arms, with its unequivocal:

'Brave, true ancient Scots... Blood untainted circled every vein.'

Wallace is remembered in a litany of more modern Scottish romantic and historical fictions, from Sir Walter Scott's *The Hero of Scotland* to Jack Whyte's *The Forest Laird*.

In 1869, the colossal Wallace monument was built overlooking the site of his most notable victory, Stirling Bridge. It still stands a towering and very permanent monument to the spirit of a hero who lies within many a Scottish heart to this day. Surveying the land he loved, from the Trossachs in the West to the Pentland Hills in the East, this Gothic landmark is a remarkable feat of Victorian engineering as well as being a Pantheon to Wallace and his fellow Scottish heroes.

There are statues to Sir William Wallace in no less than six Scottish towns. He even has a hotel bearing his name as far away as Birchgrove in New South Wales, Australia.

The Wallace Society, which has its own officially recognised tartan, has been operating since 1958. The 1995 Mel

Gibson's film *Braveheart*, which purported to represent Wallace's life, albeit with considerable artistic licence, grossed over $210 million and won five Oscars. Whatever its shortcomings, approximately 20 million people were sufficiently interested in his life to pay to hear his story told once more. And with talk of another Scottish Referendum never far below the surface of Hollyrood politics, William Wallace is perhaps as relevant now as he has ever been. To defy 'the auld enemy' in life is one thing; but to continue to defy them 715 years after you have died is truly the mark of a hero.

Perhaps the Wallace family motto simply says all that is required: *'Pro Libertate'*, 'For Freedom'.

The Wallace Monument overlooking Stirling

WILLIAM WALLACE: HERO PROFILE

Killed several English knights with his dirk or claymore

Enjoyed two 'resurrections'

Won the Battle of Stirling Bridge

Invented guerrilla warfare

Invented the Scottish schiltron

Elected Guardian of Scotland

Became the subject of a prophesy, an epic poem and a Hollywood blockbuster

Never sold out to the English

Kept the flame of Scottish Independence alive

Stood by his family motto: 'For Freedom'

Died a hero's death, defiant and dignified to the end

Became Robin Hood?

Horatio Nelson

IN AUGUST 1805, England was gripped in a frenzy of 'invasion fever'. Napoleon's revolutionary *Armée d'Angle-terre* was expected to cross the Channel at any moment: 160,000 French soldiers stared at England from the beach at Boulogne, just 25 miles across the water from Dunge-ness. The white mass of their tents could quite clearly be seen from Kent, stretching for nine miles along the coast. Its stated purpose was not to conquer England, but 'to destroy it':* a task Napoleon coldly calculated would take 'about three weeks'.

In that hysterical state, the anxious population of our islands required a saviour, a military colossus to be a bulwark against the irrepressible Bonaparte. And they seized upon the flower of the Royal Navy, the tabloid

* Earl St Vincent on Nelson.

darling of his generation, the man of the moment: that man was Horatio Nelson.

In their patriotic hero-worship they clasped him to their collective breast, almost to the point of suffocation. Pictures of him were widely sold, songs were sung of his deeds and he was mobbed in the street: 'It is beyond anything represented in a play or a poem of fame,' commented his friend Lord Minto, having just experienced being mobbed with Nelson outside a shop in Piccadilly.

Nelson himself was all too aware of the high expectations upon his shoulders:

'I am now set up for a conjurer and God knows, they will very soon find out I am far from being one,'

he wrote just weeks before his defining moment, the legendary Battle of Trafalgar.

As if in answer to their prayers and despite his own self-doubts, Nelson succeeded at Trafalgar in inflicting a crushing defeat upon the combined French and Spanish navy, thereby removing the threat of invasion from our shores at a stroke. The spectre of such a threat was not raised again for another 140 years when, in the Battle of Britain, it was once again only the heroic actions of 'the few' which saved 'the many'.

Trafalgar was a victory brought about by inspiring leadership, 'animal courage' and a self-sacrificial attitude to duty and honour. And, of course he paid the ultimate price and thereby simultaneously achieved his immortality. It was the sublime crowning glory of a true hero.

As the sixth child of a country parson and the great-grandson of a baker, there was nothing inevitable about Nelson's success. As a boy he was small and weak. He was neither academic, good at sport, nor particularly handsome. The only apparent advantage he had in life was that he had an uncle who was a sea-captain in the Royal Navy. It was an advantage he was to capitalise upon when, at only 12 years of age, he was allowed to go away to sea under his uncle's watchful eye.

Despite regularly suffering from poor health and sea-sickness, with the patronage of that uncle, his career progressed rapidly. By the age of 17 he had spent time in the West Indies, the Arctic and India. By the age of 19 he had passed his naval examinations and become an officer and in 1778, still aged only 20, he took command of his first ship. Postings in the Mediterranean, the Caribbean, the Baltic and Canada followed. But despite early successes, a combination of peace with France and an ill-advised friendship with the unpopular Duke of Clarence left him isolated from the Admiralty and miserably unemployed for over five years. Indeed, 'If the peace had lasted, the great Nelson would have been lucky ever to get a ship again, and no one would know his name.'*

Half a decade kicking his heels on half-pay perhaps partially explains his subsequent zeal for action and eagerness for a scrap whenever the chance arose.

But the French Revolution changed all that and by 1793 France had declared war on Britain. Nelson was recalled and given command of the 64-gun 'Agamemnon'. By early 1794, he was off the coast of Southern Europe under Lord Hood, seeking to gain control of the Mediterranean along the French coast. After Hood lost control of the port of Toulon, at his own suggestion, Nelson was allowed to land his ship's cannons and emplace them on the hills surrounding Bastia in Corsica. From there he was able to bombard the town into surrender, thereby temporarily giving the Royal Navy a safe port once more.

Nelson then moved on to Calvi with a view to repeating the procedure. By July, he was in position to support a planned land invasion when, leading from one of the forward batteries, an enemy shell exploded a sandbag,

* Terry Coleman: *Nelson the Man and Legend*.

causing gravel to penetrate Nelson's right eye. Although he quickly left the assault to have the eye bandaged, he returned to continue the bombardment later that day. And within a few days he stormed and captured the final French defensive position, allowing him *carte blanche* to dish out the same Nelson bombardment as he had at Bastia. On the 10th August, Calvi too surrendered and the Royal Navy had another harbour from which to patrol the French coast. It had come at the not inconsiderable cost, to Nelson, of his right eye. But, with eye-patch now defiantly in place, his immortal image was cast and ready to step up.

On the 14th February 1797, aged 39, Nelson took command of his first 74-gun battleship, 'Captain'. She was part of the British Fleet when, later that year, they encountered the much larger Spanish Fleet off Cape St Vincent in Portugal. Spain being allied to the hated French, Admiral Jervis, the fleet commander, ordered the British to attack. But as the Spanish sought to drift away under full sail, it looked as though the engagement might come to nothing. Acting on his own initiative and against his battle orders, Nelson took his own ship out of the British line and attacked the enemy at the nearest point. He broke through them on the perpendicular and drawing heavy fire he crashed his battleship into the 'San Josef'. Leading a boarding party and capitalising on the chaos his audacity had caused amongst the Spanish sailors, he took the 80-gun Spanish ship in hand-to-hand fighting. Having captured her as a prize, he immediately proceeded to repeat the manoeuvre on a second enemy ship which had come alongside and become entangled in the battle. This time it was the 112-gun 'San Nicolas'. He had invented what he was later to refer to as 'Nelson's patent bridge.'

With two first-rate battleships now under Nelson's belt, the Spanish fleet was flung into disarray. Two more Spanish battleships were taken and the others fled. Nelson's impetuosity had won the day. That tactic of 'surprise and confound' was to remain his instinctive approach to warfare thereafter. Coupled with his charm before battle and his humanity in its aftermath, it was to be his hallmark: 'The Nelson Touch'.

Nelson on the San Josef, 1797 (from the engraving by Daniel Orme)

His courage that day made him the talk of the Navy and his name had been made. Despite having had his orders ignored, Jervis was impressed by Nelson's 'transcendent zeal in the service of King and country'. In the strictly regimented hierarchy of the Royal Navy, it was perhaps fortunate for Nelson that, on this occasion, daring and single-mindedness had paid-off. In a big way. He was made a Knight of the Bath and became a rear-admiral six days later. But it was his own published account of that engagement that was largely responsible for launching Nelson's first appearance on the public stage in the role of action hero. A piece of self-publicity many of our modern-day would-be heroes would be proud of.

But the battle of Cape St Vincent was not a one-off.

Later that same year, he was instrumental in bombarding the Spanish port of Cadiz. In a sea skirmish, despite only being aboard an open ten-oared rowing boat, he fought gunwale to gunwale with three Spanish gunboats, again taking them with hand-to-hand combat. Leading with his sword and trusting in his shipmates to cover him, Nelson and his small raiding party killed or wounded so many of the Spanish crew that, overwhelmed by such naked aggression, they all surrendered. Had Nelson's coxswain not interposed his own body between his master and the Spanish sabres on at least two occasions, Nelson would have been lucky to escape with his life. As the Admiralty and members of his own family tried to remind him at the time, boarding parties were not usually lead by admirals.

But it was not all one-way traffic. Just weeks later, Nelson led a wholly unsuccessful, commando-style raid on a Spanish fortress on Tenerife. In the process, his arm was shattered by a musket ball as he went to draw his sword. By that evening the arm was amputated and, together with the blinded eye, Nelson's physical persona was set. Nelson always made light of these injuries; but they spoke louder to his men and to the public than any words. To them, it was not simply the result of his exploits which mattered, but rather the manner in which they were executed. He was the epitome of both 'leading from the front' and 'by example'. Indeed, famously, he would run up the rat-lines into the rigging shoulder to shoulder with the young midshipmen. It was an inclusive style of command which inspired.

As the eighteenth century drew to a close, all eyes looked nervously to mainland Europe and the bloody terror of revolutionary France. The one vestige of hope lay in the Royal Navy. In Nelson and some of his brother captains there rested a kind of burning quest for honour and glory which, coupled with an almost fatalistic disregard for safety, could lead to brutal and decisive engagements against the French. Indeed, Nelson genuinely believed that in these audacious attacks lay his own safety: '... *I am of the opinion that the boldest measures are the safest.*' Further, he fully appreciated that decisive naval action was what was wanted of him; or rather, what was expected. As he said to the Prime Minister of the day: '*It is, as Mr. Pitt knows, annihilation that the country wants.*' At a time when much naval activity involved long periods of tedious blockading or frustrating games of 'cat and mouse' with the enemy, Nelson had a constant appetite for 'engagement'. Speaking of the enemy fleet he exclaimed: '*I am in a fever. God send that I may find them.*' To get at them was all that he asked for.

There were other motivations. Great fortunes were to be had in prize money for those who captured valuable enemy ships. Further, Nelson had seen at first-hand the ignominy of friends and comrades who had failed to deliver. Thus, whilst he undoubtedly enjoyed the perks of fame, he was acutely aware of the inconstancy of the press. As he so perceptively observed at the time: '*Popular applause is very acceptable to me, but... it is too precarious to be depended upon.*' When, years later, he was threatened with blackmail concerning his disastrous raid on the French fleet at Boulogne, he replied with admirable hauteur: '*I have not been brought up in the school of fear and therefore care not what you do. I defy you and your malice.*'

In 1798, seven years before Trafalgar, it was widely believed that Napoleon's sights were set on Egypt and India. To stop him, Nelson had been tasked with seeking out and confronting the French fleet in the Mediterranean. It would have to be a defining encounter. But after nearly three months without a sighting of the enemy, the Admiralty were getting impatient, Britain was getting jittery and disgrace was on the horizon for Nelson. Finally, on the 1st August, he found them, anchored in line of battle off Alexandria near the mouth of the Nile. Surrounded by treacherously shallow waters and in the dangerously fading light, the French were in an apparently impregnable position.

But they had not reckoned on Nelson. No sooner were they sighted than he resolved to attack them, that very evening.

Using the wind to his advantage and sailing into perilously shallow water in order to surround them, Nelson launched an onslaught which took the French completely by surprise. Under an unremitting, two-sided bombardment, the French flagship exploded, the enemy fleet was all but destroyed and Napoleon and his army were stranded in Egypt. Only two French ships escaped capture or destruction. As usual, Nelson was left nursing another serious injury, this time a shrapnel wound to the forehead, which, had it not been for his Admiral's hat, might again have been the end of him. Years earlier he had modestly referred to the blinding of his eye as like *'a smart slap in the face'*.

Engraving of the Battle of the Nile from the 1830s

When he wrote to his wife about the battle of the Nile, he forgot to mention his head injury at all.

Such was the relief back home at this crushing defeat of Napoleon's navy that, on hearing the news, the First Lord of the Admiralty fainted. The Battle of the Nile was another example of explosive British aggression catching the enemy napping; and the British public loved it. The king made him a Baron, the government made him rich and the people lit bonfires and rang bells in his honour. The name or image of Nelson was on every conceivable piece of merchandise: Nelson medallions, snuff-boxes and Toby jugs. The phrase 'Nelson for Ever' was coined. A grateful Sultan of Turkey decorated him with the highest Turkish award for valour. The Battle of the Nile had established Nelson as the focus of British hopes against the French tyrant and as a giant in the imagination of the populace. And Nelson loved it: *'if it be a sin to covet glory, I am the most offending soul alive.'*

A pre-Nelson Emma Hamilton, as sketched by Angelica Kauffmann, 1792

So to the victor the spoils; but for Nelson there were also rewards of a more visceral nature on the horizon. Leaving Egypt for repair to body and ship, he headed to Naples. Having visited years earlier, Nelson knew he would have a warm reception there and would be welcomed with, at the very least, open arms. Despite being married, Nelson headed not to his wife but for Lady Emma Hamilton, a renowned beauty and herself wife of the British Ambassador.

Emma Hamilton had risen to her position from very humble beginnings, living on her charm and sexuality. Born to a Lancashire blacksmith, she now counted the Queen of Naples amongst her closest friends. As she admitted, she would rather 'play at all-fours' than at whist. She was the 'it girl' of her generation.

Whilst he did not press home his advantage straightaway, years later Nelson saw nothing remiss in taking Emma Hamilton openly as his own mistress and, ultimately, moving her back to England to set up home. (Indeed, four years later, Lady Hamilton gave birth to Nelson's first and only child, a daughter, Horatia.)

This personal conduct is one of many contradictions which reveal themselves throughout Nelson's life. Here he is both the honourable admiral and the ruthless adulterer: a paradox perhaps only Nelson could have got away with in the starchy Georgian society of the day.

Nelson at Palermo (drawing by Charles Grignion, 1799)

But Nelson and events were, as ever, not very far apart.

Whilst he was in Naples, rumours spread that Napoleon's army was on its way. Genuinely and understandably fearful for their lives, the King of Naples and his court begged Nelson to assist their escape to Sicily. With the mob at the palace gates, Nelson willingly obliged, rescuing the Neapolitan court and millions of pounds worth of its riches in one convoy. Only his command of his flagship, 'Vanguard', had stood between one of the royal houses of Europe and the guillotine. As he dryly observed, '*A fleet of British ships of war are the best negotiators in Europe.*' He received the title 'Duke of Bronte' for his pains. It should be remembered that Nelson was not solely a hero to the British.

By 1801, despite by now suffering from the almost inevitable fatigue and ill-health incurred after nearly thirty years at sea, Nelson was on patrol in the Baltic Sea when he determined to attack the Danish fleet at Copenhagen. Under fierce enemy bombardment from the shore, he led his ships in close to return fire. Allegedly, when signalled to call off the attack by the fleet commander, Nelson put the telescope to his blind eye and said, '*I really do not see the signal,*' a smile no doubt flickering across his lips. Instead he determined to '*give it to them till they should be sick of it.*' If this exchange was a myth, then it was a sufficiently realistic one to be credible. The aggression and the charm; the brutality and the humanity; 'The Nelson Touch' once more. For his aggression and guile on this occasion he was made a Viscount. His commanding officer was recalled and got nothing.

Where did this thirst for action come from? At a personal level, Nelson claimed to have experienced some form of patriotic vision when he was only 17, calling to him to seize his destiny or else to fade into oblivion. '*"Well then," I exclaimed, "I will be a hero and confiding in providence I will brave every danger".*' But there was also a deep-seated belligerence at play in the British psyche. That tradition, elucidated most notably in Shakespeare's *Henry*

V with the battle cry of 'Once more into the breach, dear friends...', was never far from Nelson's thinking. Indeed, he often quoted from the text of this play. But Nelson's apparent fearlessness was quite unique and he imbued it into his men. Vice-Admiral Colomb attributed to him 'a sense of duty which in religion would be called fanatical', combined with 'a sense of delight of the fox-hunting kind'. Nelson himself said of his own seamen that they '*minded shot no more than peas*'.

This British bravado and aggression was loathed and feared by our enemies in equal measure. But it was a Spaniard who so accurately summarised the position. Don Domingo Perez de Grandallana put it thus, having just witnessed the Spanish drubbing at the hands of Nelson at Cape St Vincent:

> 'An Englishman enters a naval action with the firm conviction that his duty is to hurt his enemies and help his friends... Experience shows, on the contrary that a Frenchman or a Spaniard... has no feeling for mutual support and goes into action with hesitation...'

This would appear to be a view with which Nelson sincerely concurred: '*The Dons* (Spanish) *may make fine ships,*' he said, '*they cannot however make men*'.

In 1805, after two years nervously watching Napoleon's invasion force grow across the Channel, this 'long tradition of English violence'* was moving inexorably towards a climax. Whether consciously or not, Nelson fed upon it; and his men, in their turn, were sustained through him. The people wanted violence and Nelson could deliver it. But the use of violence by Nelson was not gratuitous, neither was it relished. Indeed, he often lamented the necessity for

---

* Adam Nicholson: *Men of Honour.*

the horror of warfare and his sensitivity is illustrated by his disgust at the 'sport' of bull-fighting, regarding it simply as '*too much*'. That gentleness of spirit is echoed by his approach to surgery aboard ship. Only Nelson insisted that his surgeons warm their knives before Trafalgar, to mitigate the pain of the cold steel as it did its work.

By the same token, Nelson, more than anyone, was eager to act with decency and kindness in the horrific aftermath of battle. Praying just hours before Trafalgar, it was not violence or courage for which he pleaded, but *'for humanity to be the predominant feature in the British fleet'*. The iron fist followed by the velvet glove. That nobility of spirit was what bound his crew and his officers to him: his 'Band of Brothers', as he referred to them (again quoting *Henry V*).

And undoubtedly Nelson had talismanic status amongst his fleet. The prime factor in the Trafalgar victory was attributed to 'the enthusiasm inspired throughout the British fleet from their being commanded by their beloved Nelson' (Lieutenant Senhouse). Or as Lord Collingwood put it after Trafalgar: 'There is nothing like him left for gallantry and conduct in battle,' and 'Everything seemed, as if by enchantment, to prosper under his direction.' Reading from the personal diaries and letters of seamen of all ranks, written immediately prior to that battle, the one common thread is their respect for and belief in their commander. Commenting upon Nelson's arrival at the British fleet in the days preceding Trafalgar, an able-seaman wrote, 'It is impossible to describe the heartfelt satisfaction… and the confidence of success with which we were inspired.'

But by the spring of 1805, Napoleon's *armies* were still unbeaten and the French invasion of England was no pie in the sky. The greatest amphibious military operation ever contemplated was poised for action. The French army had begun to march down to the beach at Boulogne for disembarkation. Indeed, on the 22nd August 1805, Napoleon expressly ordered the commander of the French navy to: 'Make a start. Lose not a moment and come into the Channel, bringing our united squadrons, and England is ours. We are ready; everything is embarked. Be here but for twenty-four hours and all is ended.' Had the French navy shown-up, the invasion would have started. That is how close things were, because in order to effect this mass-invasion, the French convoys required protection from the Royal Naval Fleet in the Channel.

To this end, an 'armada' of French and Spanish ships of the line had been amassed. Currently those ships lay blockaded in various French and Spanish ports. But in order to shake off the British garrison fleet at Cadiz, the bulk of the Combined Fleet was to slip off to the West Indies, where they would re-group. The plan for the French was to send Nelson off on a wild goose-chase looking for them, regroup in the West Indies and then sweep back into the Channel to deliver the '*manœuvre sur les derrières*', as Napoleon termed it. With 60 French and Spanish ships 'sweeping the Channel', the remnants of the Royal Navy would be powerless to protect its own shores. The Channel would be wide open. Julius Caesar, William the Conqueror and now Napoleon.

But Napoleon did not count on Nelson's tenacity. Having got wind of their departure, Nelson followed the enemy fleet all the way to Jamaica and then back again, a round trip of some 6,686 miles. In so doing, he almost certainly averted a wholesale sacking of the British West Indies. When he finally caught up with the French again, they had, after a skirmish with Admiral Calder's fleet off Cape Finisterre, returned to the safety of Cadiz. Whilst far from decisive, that skirmish had at least diverted the enemy from the Channel and so, for the time being Nelson was off the hook. But he could not countenance them '*giving him the slip*' a second time. Equally, another inconclusive skirmish would not be tolerated. With southern England braced for the second Gallic conquest of the millennium, the next encounter *had* to be decisive.

In fact, that skirmish and the shilly-shallying of the French navy delayed the invasion and caused Napoleon, in his frustration, to turn his attentions to Eastern Europe. The French had missed their chance. However, even by late summer, it was still widely believed that the invasion of Britain was imminent. And the only way to avoid it and to restore calm was by a decisive and devastating victory over the Combined French and Spanish fleet. '*An annihilating victory*' was how Nelson saw it. '*When we meet, God be with us, for we must not part again till one fleet or other is totally destroyed.*' No pressure, then.

It was in that atmosphere that the country looked to Nelson. For all his hat-waving and smiles, as he set off from the George Hotel in Portsmouth to take up his command aboard Victory on the 14th September 1805, he must have suspected that this was to be the final roll of the dice. Indeed, days before he left England for the last time, he had arranged for his name to be engraved upon his coffin.

The story of Trafalgar is an epic in itself and cannot be done justice to here.

But in short form, this is how it went. Whilst keeping the Combined Fleet under observation in Cadiz harbour, it was clear that Nelson's fleet was significantly outnumbered. Equally, most of its ships had been at sea continuously for two years. But there was no question of his worrying about this numerical mismatch: quite the contrary. In the weeks leading to that inevitable confrontation, Nelson chose to reduce the number of his fleet still further, thereby trying to tempt the French out of port. Only days before the battle, he had sent six British war-ships to Gibraltar for re-victualling, knowing full well that they would in all likelihood miss the battle altogether. It wasn't beating the enemy that was Nelson's concern, it was getting at them. That his sailors were long overdue a rest did not concern him either. Rather, he knew that two years at sea had made them fit, hungry and experienced. Even if his ships were in worse repair than he would have liked, at least his crews knew exactly how to sail them.

Nelson's little ruse worked. Intelligence that the six British ships had left was not long in getting to the French commander, Villeneuve. As much as he dreaded the prospect of a show-down with Nelson, he realised the odds were as good now as they were ever likely to be; and so he came out. Ostensibly, he was heading for the Mediterranean. But he must have known what was about to happen. His officers did not spend the day saying their prayers for nothing.

As the British fleet pursued the enemy off Cape Trafalgar on the 21st October 1805, numerically the odds were with the combined Fleet. They had 33 ships to our 27.

But Nelson had an audacious plan and one he could barely wait to put into effect. Rather than fight a conventional naval battle, with the two sides passing each other in two parallel lines and blasting their broadsides into each other until one submitted, Nelson decided to attack the enemy at right angles, breaking their line with two closely grouped columns. Having broken through, he would then allow his captains to take on the enemy ships one by one, spontaneously, explosively and, hopefully decisively. *'It will bring forward a pell-mell battle and that is what I want,'* he said. It is in effect what he did personally at Cape St Vincent, but on a huge and orchestrated scale. As he replied to his second in command, Captain Hardy, as they came within firing distance of the enemy lines; when asked which particular ship they should engage first, he answered: *'Go on board which you please. Take your choice!'* In other words, it matters not: fight them and beat them one by one. As he concluded in his final memorandum to his captains, *'no Captain can do very wrong if he places his ship alongside that of an enemy.'* This was the ethos which overwhelmed the Combined Fleet at Trafalgar. The unleashing of spontaneous, zealous and uncompromising violence by each one of his captains, wherever they saw the opportunity.

Nelson realised, both instinctively and pragmatically, that he had to lead from the front. He knew full well that the tone of the battle would be set in the first encounters. The enemy line needed to be punched hard by the best ships with the most experienced commanders. Thus it was Nelson and Collingwood who were to lead the charge in their respective flag-ships, Victory and Royal Sovereign. He knew that where he led, others would follow; the rest of the engagement could be left to the collective initiative and bravery of the Royal Navy.

As he led his column into battle, in a sense he had already done his job. The die had been cast. Of the mighty ships of the line which followed their admirals into that bloody fray – 'Colossus', 'Revenge', 'Defiance', 'Dreadnought', 'Leviathan', 'Thunderer' – not one of them pulled their punches, backed their sails or stood off to see how things turned out. That was the difference between the two navies and between the national characters of the men who manned them. As an able seaman so powerfully put it, the question was 'whether the boasted heroism of France and Spain or the genuine valour of free born Britons was to rule the Main.' Trafalgar was the unequivocal answer to that riddle.

Despite Nelson's meticulous planning and the simplicity of the general concept, it seems that on the day, adrenalin got the better of him. Having told the ships to advance tightly-bunched for maximum effect, Nelson himself could not wait for stragglers to catch up. Further, instead of waiting for the 'Temeraire' to draw parallel and at least share the brunt of those opening salvoes as the ships entered into the killing zone, as had been agreed, he insisted on 'Victory' pulling ahead with every inch of canvass out to dry. 'Lord Nelson's anxiety to close with the enemy became very apparent,' wrote one of his officers afterwards. As he watched Lord Collingwood's division crash into the enemy line just ahead and to starboard of him, he could barely contain himself. The stump of his right arm, his 'fin', jerked with anticipation. '*See how that noble fellow Collingwood carries his ship into action,*' he said, no doubt trying to keep a lid on his jealousy. And Collingwood could read his thoughts; watching Victory across the rolling Atlantic swell, he gloated to one of his officers, 'Rotherham, what would Nelson give to be here?' What Nelson would give was this: *'I'll give them such a dressing as they never had before'*. Such was he heard to mutter as he surveyed the enemy sails through his tele-scope. One can still almost feel the electric atmosphere on those rolling quarter-decks. Any attempt to shorten sail and allow the 'Temeraire' to draw level was met with vitriol from the Admiral. Instead, whether in the heat of the moment or as a deliberate and typically Nelsonian gesture, he resolved that his flagship would crash through the enemy line ahead of his column, thus drawing the most fearful pounding. The danger to himself and his crew was inescapable.

Perhaps he simply could not bear the tension a moment longer. It is one of the ironies of war, particularly of such an inevitably bloody and furious battle as was imminent, that peace can, in some ways, only be found in the thick of it. The apprehension and nerves in the days leading up to the battle must have been intolerable. The responsibility and expectation upon his shoulders, insufferable. But once immersed in the organised chaos of battle there could be no more worry. Simply death or glory. Somewhat paradox-ically again, for Nelson it was only in the very crucible of battle that he could find peace.

It has often been suggested that this headlong plunge into the enemy line was a kind of death-wish: a deliber-ate and final act of self-sacrifice. There is certainly some support for such a contention. Why else would he insist, against the advice of his trusted friend Captain Hardy, upon wearing his four Orders of Knighthood upon his tail-coat, so clearly visible to the enemy snipers as he strode around the deck, refusing to take any form of cover? Why else would he have driven his own ship on, away from his own fleet and away from his own plan, to take the brunt of those early murderous onslaughts? And why else would he say to his friend, Captain Henry Blackwood, as the cannon balls started to fly, *'God bless you, Blackwood, I shall never speak to you again.'*

Indeed, it could be said that the very concept of the battle-plan itself was semi-suicidal. It was a deliberate course of reckless, anarchic violence, at whatever the cost. To run at the enemy, fully exposed to their broadsides, to break their line and then to attack them at close quarters was, however things went, going to be a bloodbath for HMS 'Victory'.

As the two fleets drifted inexorably together, the signal flags flew: *'England expects every man will do his duty.'* It is one of the most famous lines ever communicated in the English language; and one of the most frequently repeated. As an understated battle cry, it is inspirational. And that must have been its effect as it was signalled from battleship to battleship; each time received with roars and hurrahs from intoxicated crews. And as those British cheers drifted downwind across the waves; as the French and Spanish waited for hell to be unleashed upon them, the intimidation of those less experienced sailors within the enemy fleet can only be guessed at.

And hell it was to be. 'A murderous punch delivered at about walking pace' is how Adam Nicolson brilliantly describes the unstoppable giants of the British fleet as they drifted towards the enemy line on the light breeze and rolling swells. The opening broadside from 'Royal Sovereign's' 40 cannon, which raked through the decks of 'Santa Ana', allegedly killed 400 men in one fell swoop.

However many casualties there were in reality, there could be no recovery from that scale of onslaught and the battle could only go one way.

In the ensuing maelstrom of gunfire, there were a multitude of heroic and tragic dramas played out on both sides. Indeed, at times the battle was delicately poised. But despite heroic efforts by many of the enemy battleships, after four hours of unremitting fire-fighting, whereas an astounding 17 enemy ships had been captured and one destroyed, not one British ship had 'struck its colours'. The remainder of the Combined Fleet wisely fled for their lives. Some 3,000 enemy sailors had been killed to only 449 British. It was the greatest naval rout in history and its legacy was to secure Britain's pre-eminence at sea for at least another 100 years. 'Winning was Nelson's genius and he had won.'* But it was not simply Nelson's strategy which had won Trafalgar. It was Nelson's charisma.

It won Britain 'the empire of the ocean' and that in due course built the British empire itself. But more importantly at the time, it was the perceived end of Napoleonic ambitions, at least in our direction. It would be left to Wellington to finish him off, once and for all, 10 years later.

Ultimately, Trafalgar was the personification of all things Nelsonian. It was audacity, it was bravery, it was honour and ultimately it was victory. But it was also slaughter, recklessness and, as it turned out, near-disaster. For Britain, however, it was the quintessence of violent defiance which has remained in the patriotic imagination ever since: a bloody Arcadia; Britannia's terrible climax.

Of course, the glorious tragedy was that amongst the hundreds of British corpses, lay Nelson himself. As he had predicted to Captain Hardy as the intensity of the battle was unleashed, '*This is too hot work to last long.*' Almost inevitably, Nelson's virtually suicidal tactics extracted the ultimate sacrifice. He was shot by a French sniper from a range of only 50 yards. Insisting on promenading the quarter-deck in full view and in his distinctive and heavily decorated Admiral's coat, the only surprise is that he was

* Terry Coleman: *Nelson the Man and Legend.*

not hit sooner. The musket ball had bisected his body from left epaulette to the base of his spine. That he survived as long as he did was remarkable. But his body held on just long enough to hear those 17 enemy ships 'strike their colours'. The cheers were British and the day was Nelson's. He had been a martyr to a victorious cause.

His final words were not, as is often thought, '*Kiss me Hardy…*' but rather, '*Thank God I have done my duty,*' muttered again and again until his breath ran out.

The death of Nelson was depicted in many ways, including this simple but popular print from around 1810.

Having been returned to England, preserved in the famous rum barrel, he was interred at St Paul's Cathedral in the largest single ceremony that emblematic dome has ever witnessed. Women were not invited.

The Right Honourable, Lord Viscount Nelson KB, Duke of Bronte in Sicily, Knight of the Great Cross of St Ferdinand and of Merit, Knight of the Order of the Crescent and of the illustrious Order of St Joachim, Vice-Admiral of the White and Commander-in-Chief of his Majesty's ships and vessels. The weedy boy from Burnham Thorpe had come a long way.

But Horatio Lord Nelson is more than simply the post-humous victor of the defining sea battle of modern times. He remains the most inspiring heroic paradox of our nation's history. Pirate-admiral, romantic-adulterer, egotistical man-of-the-people, gentleman-predator; a quixotic man of contradictions, the epitome of the flawed genius. 'He is in many points a really great man; in others a baby,' reflected Lord Minto.

Ultimately, his own personal tragedy was simultaneously the summit of his heroic achievement. To die at the very point of victory preserved him as a hero in his prime. He quit life whilst he was at its very zenith and simultaneously realised his own spiritual ambition: *'a glorious death is to be envied'*. Indeed, his timing was, in some ways, impeccable. For no sooner had his spirit left him than the barometer off Cape Trafalgar plummeted, plunging the Fleet into a storm which raged for five days and claimed more lives and many more ships than the battle itself. Many of those who endured the chaos of that terrifying tempest must have harboured envious thoughts of their recently departed hero, resting as he was in eternal peace.

'The Martyred Mariner'; to Byron he was 'Britannia's God of War.' Over 200 years on, one can still drink a toast to him in one of the 250 public houses which honour his name and exploits. As he still stands 185 feet above London today, he remains the pre-eminent hero of our entire island history. His is literally the tallest plinth in the pantheon. As James Muirden recently put it:

> 'His eye was smashed beyond repair
> And his arm was blown to bits.
> But he's up in the air in Trafalgar Square,
> Way above all the rest of the Brits!'

Indeed. For his fearlessness, dash and sheer patriotism, he epitomises the very core of British defiance at its most formidable.

HORATIO NELSON: HERO PROFILE

Adopted commando tactics and engaged in hand-to-hand fighting when an Admiral

Boarded two enemy battleships simultaneously at Cape St Vincent ('Nelson's patent bridge')

Rewrote the rules of engagement at sea

Destroyed the Napoleonic Fleet in Egypt

Thrashed the Combined French and Spanish Fleet at Trafalgar

He had a veritable litany of quotations attributable to him, such as: 'Gentlemen, when the enemy is committed to a mistake, we must not interrupt him too soon.'

Severely wounded to eye, arm and head without making a fuss.

Issued the defining battle cry of 'England expects...'

Loved by his men

Adored by 'the most beautiful woman in Europe', Lady Emma Hamilton

Placed duty and honour before personal safety

Died in the thick of battle

Arthur Wellesley
The Iron Duke

ARTHUR WELLESLEY IS the personification of understated British military supremacy. Through his gargantuan efforts and those of the men he led, he was able to weaken the French empire and ultimately to defeat the egotistical Napoleon.

His calm dignity, unflinching bravery and bursts of savage courage literally changed the course of world history.

Arthur Wesley (as his name is recorded on his birth certificate) was born in Dublin on the 1st May 1769. He was always a little sensitive about his Irish background, insisting that he was English. As he pointed out in typically blunt language, '*being born in a barn doesn't make somebody a horse!*' For somebody so celebrated for thrashing the French, it is ironic that in fact his own

Anglo-Irish family were descended from Norman nobility granted lands in Britain by the French Duke, William the Conqueror.

As a boy and young man Arthur was idle and lacking in any apparent distinction. He hated his time at Eton because he was lonely and by his own admission 'learnt nothing'. It is thus highly unlikely that he ever uttered the words, 'The Battle of Waterloo was won on the playing fields of Eton.' This is particularly so as at the time Eton in fact had no playing fields. His education in England was curtailed and he was sent instead to an Academy in France where, if nothing else, he at least became fluent in French.

As he grew up, one of the few things he did like was playing the violin. Indeed, he would do this to the exclusion of almost everything else, particularly his academic studies. However, such was his resolve to join the military that, demonstrating commendable self-awareness, he decided to burn his violin so that it could no longer act as a distraction: an extreme but effective early career decision. However, that natural love of music never left him and in much later life, the old Duke was the proud owner of the first English grand piano, which he was highly accomplished at playing and which is still to be found at his old Mayfair Town House: Number One, London.

He also developed a liking for a young lady by the name of Kitty Packenham. However, when he asked her to marry, her brother, the Earl of Longford, refused him, opining that Arthur was 'a young man with very poor prospects.' His father having died when Arthur was a boy, his mother was left to worry as to her son's future, saying, 'I don't know what I shall do with my awkward son.'

Soldier

What he did was join the army. Coming from an aristocratic family, a commission was easily purchased and he became an Ensign at the age of 18. He enjoyed his military life well enough, for by the age of twenty-seven he had risen to colonel. But it was not until he was sent to India in 1797 that things really started to hot-up for him.

An 1890s illustration of Wellesley before the Battle of Assaye

His command was tasked with extending the control of the British East India Company. However, with many of the local Sultanates supported by the French, this led to a series of conflicts. Being the brother of the Governor General of the day, Arthur had both the opportunity and the determination to excel. At the Battle of Assaye in 1803, he was described as 'being in the thick of the action the whole time.' Outnumbered ten to one, he had two horses shot from under him. But despite losing the horses he won the battle, which he often rated as his greatest ever victory. Soon after, he was at the Battle of Argaum, where the British army took 5,000 enemy lives at a cost of just

361 to themselves. These two victories paved the way to a peace settlement with the Sultans, which was good for trade and good for the Empire. Wesley, who at his brother's instigation had now re-fashioned his name to the more elegant 'Wellesley', had distinguished himself and in 1804 he was made a Knight of the Bath and soon returned to England. His military reputation had not gone unnoticed; as Napoleon Bonaparte commented at the time, 'This is a man with whom I shall have to deal.' Indeed.

Interestingly, now that he was knighted and had a fortune in prize-money under his belt, the Earl of Longford and the Packenham family decided that Wellesley's prospects were not so poor after all and he was finally allowed to marry Kitty.

After a short time dabbling in politics, he was sent to the Iberian Peninsula as a Major-General. This was a long and bloody campaign against the French revolutionary armies in which Wellesley's true military gifts emerged. Most notably, he won the battles of Porto, Talavera and Salamanca, in which he routed the French and returned Madrid to Spanish control. Joseph Bonaparte, Napoleon's brother, was deposed from the Spanish throne and as Wellesley's tally of defeated French generals lengthened, his reputation soared. He campaigned tirelessly. He personally led the attack against the French at the Battle of Vitoria, a victory about which Beethoven composed his Opus 114. The fact that the British captured 137 out of 138 French guns is some indication of the success of this battle. With the French army in retreat, he invaded Southern France, ultimately taking Toulouse and precipitating Napoleon's first abdication in 1814.

In all of those six years in Spain and Portugal, he had lost not one battle, nor so much as one British cannon. He had also taken no time off. Wellesley was not a man for holidays in the sun.

Battle of Salamanca (1812); engraving made in 1815

On his return to England after six years of successful but unremitting conflict in the Iberian campaign, he was promoted to Viscount, Earl, Marquis and Duke all at once. The upshot was that Arthur Wellesley KG, KP, GCB, GCH, PC, FRS had by now become the Duke of Wellington, Marquis Douro, Earl of Mornington, Viscount Wellesley, Baron Mornington and Douro. In due course, he was also granted titles from three foreign countries, making him the Prince of Waterloo (from the Dutch), Duque de Ciudad Rodrigo (from the Spanish) and Duque de Vitória, Marquês de Torres Vedras and Conde de Vimeiro (from the Portuguese): a frenzy of honours and titles. He had also become a General and Field Marshal during the campaign. The swearing-in ceremony took an entire day. From a grateful nation he received the country estate of Stratfield Saye in Hampshire. But Wellington needed a London house as well and Apsley House on Hyde Park Corner fitted the bill. As the first house past the toll-gate from the West, it is known as 'Number One, London' to this day. As addresses go it is hard to beat. It is the last remaining great London town house, still housing a magnificent collection of paintings and furniture and remains the London address of the Wellesley family.

Waterloo

But neither Wellington nor Napoleon had finished yet. After his first defeat and abdication, the disgraced French Emperor had been sent to the island of Elba, off the West coast of Italy. However, he was still far from unpopular with the rank and file of the 'Grand Armée' and on the 26th February 1815 he managed to escape to the mainland. By May he had re-established control of a hastily re-assembled French army. It was a gathering of 120,000 patriotic, Bonapartist veterans. Desperate to confront him but with much of the old Peninsular army now in America, Britain quickly created a European alliance, including Dutch, German and Prussian forces. The Duke of Wellington was sent to command that allied force in an attempt to bring the French to heel for a second time.

By June, the French army was on the rampage, advancing into Belgium and routing the Prussians at Ligny. After some bruising but inconclusive engagements at Quatre Bras on the 16th, on Sunday the 18th June the British and French armies finally met. Napoleon and Wellington faced each other across the open corn fields just south of the village of Waterloo. This was the one and only time these two great generals met on the field of battle. The outcome would dictate the fate of Europe. Napoleon was supremely confident as he observed the British army, spread out along the ridge. 'I tell you Wellington is a bad General, that the English are bad troops and this is going to be a picnic,' Napoleon bragged. He even ordered mutton for a celebratory dinner to be held in Brussels that night. Wellington had a very different take on proceedings, *'The French are going to get the devil of a surprise when they see how I defend a position.'* Waterloo was Wellington's chance to dispatch Napoleon once and for all; he wasn't going to squander it.

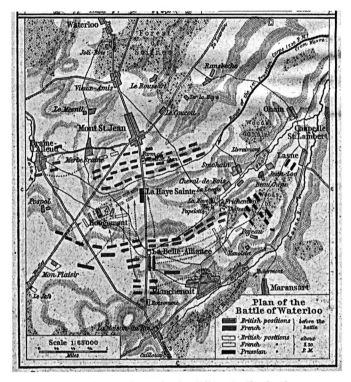

Battle map of Waterloo by William R. Shepherd

I am not even going to attempt to describe the events of that world-changing battle. Many learned and excellent books have been written on the subject, from such eminent authors as Victor Hugo in *Les Misérables* and Brendan Simm in *The Longest Afternoon*. Its complexity, atrocity and scale are themselves the stuff of legend. But, in essence, the British line was hinged around two farmsteads; Hougoumont and Le Haye Saint. To dislodge them, Napoleon decided upon a withering artillery bombardment in an attempt to break Wellington's right flank. Having done so, anticipating a migration in the British line to plug the gap, he intended to launch an all-out infantry assault on the allied left-centre to divide the British army in two. But Napoleon had underestimated the British. Firstly, Wellington had placed most of his army on the 'reverse slope', partially hiding them and providing some degree of protection from the bombardment. Secondly, despite the withering onslaught, the well-disciplined and plucky British line just managed to hold. As the French infantry advanced, they were scythed down by the heroic charges of the British cavalry, albeit at massive cost to those illustrious regiments. As Wellington reorganized his line, Marshal Ney misread it as a retreat and attacked with cavalry of his own, finally bisecting the British.

With the line now fractured, the British infantry regiments were forced to adopt their legendary defensive squares which were now subjected to twelve repeated cavalry charges and an unremitting series of merciless artillery bombardments. The British position was desperate. But of a perfectly reasonable request to withdraw for cover from one of his own officers Wellington replied, '*He and I, and every other Englishman on the field must stand and die on the spot that we occupy.*' The squares held. Desperate to gain control of the battle before the imminent arrival of the Prussian army, the French launched a final attack and managed to capture Hougoumont, one of the key farmsteads on the British line. The British withdrew and the French sensed victory. Urgently pressing home his advantage again, Napoleon played his ace card and ordered the Imperial Guard to advance and annihilate the British retreat. But Wellington was ahead of him. He coolly watched the Imperial Guard advance until they were, in some cases only 40 meters away from the British line.

If any one moment in the battle defined the disciplined and courageous defiance of the British soldier, it was at this moment, as they stood their ground, without returning fire as the Imperial Guard bore down upon them. That Wellington held his nerve and could inspire his men to do likewise is the mark of the man. And he rewarded them for their trust. As the range between the two armies reached point-blank, Wellington raised his hat to signal the release of a terrible British fusillade of mixed arms fire. Simultaneously he ambushed the French on their left flank with hidden infantry cross-fire. The over-cocky French faltered, and capitalising on their disarray, Wellington launched a desperate but deliberate counter-attack, forcing the French to retreat and then flee in undisciplined panic. As Wellington modestly later admitted, *'I never saw the British infantry behave so well.'* Almost simultaneously, Britain's Prussian allies under General von Blucher had arrived, containing the French reinforcements and dashing any remaining hope Napoleon may have had to re-group. Whatever role the Prussians played in that epic and historic victory, there can be no doubt that they arrived just in the nick of time as far as the exhausted and depleted Allied soldiers were concerned.

Wellington's artillery at Waterloo
(engraving by Geo Jones, 1816)

Napoleon was caught between a rock and a hard place and his army fled. Wellington graciously allowed the Prussians the pleasure of pursuing the French army all the way back to France. As he contemptuously scoffed, 'I have seen their backs before…' By the end of that Sunday, the French had lost approximately half of their entire army. The cost to the allies had also been horrendous. Over half of all the British infantry officers in action that day lay dead. Nine murderous hours had felled 50,000 men on one battlefield.

Far from being an occasion for celebration, the aftermath of the battle left its witnesses horrified. 'The field of battle next morning presented a frightful scene of carnage; it seemed as if the world had tumbled to pieces and three-fourths of everything destroyed in the wreck' (John Kincaid of the 95th rifles). Wellington's spirits reflected the horrendous human cost. On his return to Brussels he stated simply, *'Do not congratulate me. I have lost all my friends.'* It was in this horrendous post-traumatic melancholy that he wrote the profound, '*I always say that, next to a battle lost the greatest misery is a battle gained.'*

But at least Napoleon had been well and truly dealt with and had no choice but to surrender. He was forced to abdicate, embarrassingly for a second time and threw himself on the mercy of the British, who above all nationalities he much admired. Like all bullies, he respected only those who stood up to him. Rather than executing him, as he so richly deserved, he was transported to the tiny island of St Helena, in the middle of the Atlantic Ocean, where he remained until he died; a military genius; a world-changing egomaniac; a bitter and angry man.

Waterloo was one of the most decisive battles in history. Not only did it rid Europe of 'Boney', the bogey-man who had intimidated an entire European generation; but it also represented the end of the French Revolution. The Bourbon kings would soon be back on the throne of France, albeit not for long. But Wellington, a man of duty to the end, stayed on in France for three more years, commander of the allied army of occupation. He treated the vanquished French with respect. He spoke their language, enjoyed their culture and even, showing commendable adaptability, adopted a couple of Napoleon's abandoned mistresses as his own. By all accounts the Englishman was the more vigorous lover. But by 1818 the taste of France was starting to sour and Wellesley returned to England. It was time for Wellington to hang up his boots.

> 'For this is England's greatest son,
> He that gain'd a hundred fights
> Nor ever lost an English gun.'

Statesman

On his return to England after Waterloo, much as Nelson had been 10 years earlier, he was fêted as the saviour of Europe. Peace was expected and after an exhausting career in the army, Wellington decided to go into politics. He had already dabbled earlier in his career, becoming an Irish MP and then an English MP back in 1806. By 1828 he had become Prime Minister of a Tory government. However, he refused to live in No 10 Downing Street, because he thought the house was 'too small'. This uncompromising sense of style was echoed in his personal habits.

One of his nicknames was 'The Beau' on account of his rather dashing dress sense. He didn't much care for the new lower-class breed of parliamentarians entering the House of Commons, commenting, *'I never saw so many shocking bad hats in my life.'* Also, as far as he was concerned, the fact that he was Prime Minister in no way stopped him challenging the Earl of Winchelsea to a duel in Battersea Park, which he did on the 21st March 1829. The Earl refused to take aim and so, it is said, the Duke deliberately fired wide. It was either that or he missed a stationary target at 20 paces, which seems unlikely.

In later years his popularity waned, largely on account of his unmitigated conservatism. His opposition to the Reform Acts led to the windows of his London house being put in. It was the installation of metal shutters to protect them that earned him the waggish nick-name of 'the Iron Duke'.

He also had a reputation for being a little aloof and unfriendly, particularly to those of an inferior social standing – which unfortunately included almost everybody. He refused to speak to his valet, communicating his orders only by written messages left on his dressing table. Indeed, he was a true product of the rigidly class-bound society of early 19th-century England. Although he had generally provided well for his soldiers, he had been exceedingly strict and after the Battle of Vitoria, disgusted at their pillaging and drunkenness, referring to them in this way: *'We have in the service the scum of the earth as common soldiers.'* He was not much more polite about the cavalry regiments he commanded, opining that they appeared to be totally incapable of successfully manoeuvring, *'except on Wimbledon Common'*. Indeed, even after the heroic albeit suicidal cavalry charges at Waterloo, he commented, 'The only things that they can be relied on to do is to gallop too far and too fast!'

For all his virtues, perhaps the common touch was not one of them. That being said, he did have the humble Wellington boot named after him. His veteran troops at Waterloo fondly referred to him as 'our Atty' or 'Old Nosey'. And only Nelson can posthumously lay claim to having had more pubs named after him and his many victories. And there were, occasionally traces of humility too: 'When other Generals make mistakes, their armies are beaten. When I get into a hole, my men pull me out of it.'

The man

He usually got up early because he *'couldn't bear to lie in,'* routinely sleeping for six hours or less. He preferred to eat cold meat and bread and even when not on campaign, preferred to sleep on a camp bed, eschewing creature comforts. He often forwent lunch altogether. But wine he liked and he drank it, bottle at a time.

Although generally lacking in outward signs of emotion, he was prone to the occasional outburst. Just before the battle of Salamanca, he was eating a chicken leg whilst simultaneously examining the French flank through his telescope. As he watched he noticed a weak link in the enemy line and realised that he could launch a successful attack. Throwing the drumstick in the air, he shouted '*Les Français sont perdus*!' ('The French are lost!') And he was quite right.

Sketch by Millais of Wellington's funeral, 1852

The Duke of Wellington retired from his life in parliament in 1846. He stayed on as Commander-in-Chief of the Army, having replaced the 'Grand old Duke of York' (of nursery rhyme infamy) in that role and kept various honorary posts until he died at Walmer Castle in 1852 at the grand old age of 83. He was buried in St Paul's Cathedral on 16th November 1852, side-by-side with Lord Nelson (who, prior to his internment, he had only ever met once before). He was honoured with the last ever heraldic state funeral held in this country. Alfred Lord Tennyson commemorated the event in his poem, 'Ode on the Death of the Duke of Wellington'. His old regiment, the 33rd foot, have been known as the 'Duke of Wellington's' ever since. In more modern times, he has had two RAF Vickers bombers named after him, the 'Wellesley' and the 'Wellington' and also a World War I Battleship, 'Iron Duke'.

> 'Now to the roll of muffled drums
> To Thee the greatest soldier comes.'

Epitaph

After his death, there was an outpouring of national grief which manifested itself in the building of many monuments, public buildings and statues. Wellington College, four Wellington Monuments and Waterloo station are just a few of them; the last a perverse memorial bearing in mind he hated trains. The capital of New Zealand is also called Wellington in his honour although, regrettably, he never had time to visit.

Two hundred years on, there are still a staggering 122 roads in Greater London alone named after the Duke and his derring-do.

In all his military campaigning, Wellington had demonstrated meticulous planning, great personal bravery and brilliant defensive strategy. Interspersed with bursts of intense aggression and the employment of daring counter-attacks, they are the qualities which made him the most revered soldier in our nation's history. Of the sixty battles in his career, he didn't lose a single one. That is why his officers felt that, 'while he was there, nothing could go wrong.'

> 'Let the mournful... music blow,
> The last great Englishman is low.'

ARTHUR WELLESLEY: HERO PROFILE

Thrashed the French innumerable times

Caused Napoleon to abdicate; twice

Won the most famous victory in British military history: Waterloo

Subdued the Indian sub-continent

Had a poem and an opus written about him

Was prime minister; twice

Coined such jingoistic quotations as: 'We always have been, we are and I hope we always shall be detested in France'

Had almost as many pubs named after him and his battles as Lord Nelson

Is the most popular street name in London

Hated school

Captain Albert Ball VC

THE FIRST EVER British flying 'Ace', Albert Ball shot down dozens of enemy aircraft over the trenches of the First World War before crashing into a Flanders field and dying in the arms of a young French girl.

> 'As an example of sustained courage, displayed over many months in the face of acute danger, the record of Captain Albert Ball... will surely never be surpassed.'

That is the opinion of General Sir Peter de la Billière in his book *Supreme Courage*. And as former head of the British army, he should know.

One of Ball's colleagues described him as 'the offspring of a vixen and a lion' , who '... did the work of a whole squadron by himself'. He was 'utterly fearless and uncommunicative… he was a self-effacing, skilled and dedicated killer…'

He was also very much his own man. At boarding school in Grantham, feeling a little homesick, he once built his own boat which he sailed home by river and canal all the way to Nottingham. On another occasion, he disappeared from school and was found in the engine room of a Liverpool steamer, stowed away and about to put to sea.

He was dashingly good-looking, although not in the clichéd matinee idol sense. Rather, he was 'short and slight, beautifully proportioned, with black hair and a rosy complexion almost of the kind one would associate with a girl.' But, if he was superficially angelic, as far as the Germans were concerned, he was to become a kind of angel of death.

The Great War broke out shortly after his 18th birthday. He immediately volunteered, joining the Sherwood Foresters Regiment, romantically known as the 'Robin Hoods'. Within a couple of months he was promoted to officer rank. A chance posting to London encouraged him to take flying lessons at Hendon.

This had twin incentives for Ball: the sheer excitement of actually flying, an activity which was still in its infancy, coupled with the prospect of becoming a pilot in the newly formed Royal Flying Corps (predecessor of the RAF). This promised a rapid transfer to the front and active service in France. This was a determined plan by Ball as he confided to his father in a letter, '… *if the country is very short of pilots, I shall be able to go.*' With his own money and by taking lessons before breakfast, he finally obtained his certificate. On the 17th February 1916 he was posted to No.13 Squadron in France and this heroic figure literally took off.

It should not be forgotten that flying in the BE2 bi-planes at this stage was an incredibly primitive affair and the planes were primarily intended for reconnaissance purposes. The pilot was in an open cockpit, the machine gun provided had to be aimed outside the arc of the propeller and there was rarely any ground to air communication. Bombs were literally tossed manually out of the cockpit as one might throw an apple-core out of the window of a car driving along a motorway today. Equally, the planes were absurdly unreliable and their engines often failed. Flying at only 70 mph, they were also easy targets for anti-aircraft fire. Quite inconceivable by today's standards, Ball endured his entire flying career without ever being provided with a parachute. But Ball spent little time dwelling on such Health and Safety considerations, it would seem.

A 'Blériot Experimental' (BE) biplane

By contrast, the German 'Fokkers' were agile monoplanes, with machine guns synchronised to fire through the propeller rotation and a overall top speed fifty percent greater than the British planes. But this inequality of arms did not deter Ball who flew aggressively from the start, taking on the superior enemy planes and then, on returns from sorties, deliberately flying low over enemy lines to 'shoot up' the German trenches as well. He defined the birth of a new type of hero, the first ever 'fighter pilots', a term which did not exist until he came along. As far as aerobatics, formation and the tactics of engagement were concerned, they were left to Ball and his colleagues to develop on their own. It was trial and error at its most extreme.

The first Fokker 'Eindecker' (E.II), 1915

Ball's signature manoeuvre was to drop down behind a German aircraft, come up into its blind spot and then rake his machine gun along the enemy's underbelly from an unfeasibly close distance, sometimes as little as 15 yards. Lethal for the enemy and fraught with danger for Ball. He was also the first ever pilot to think of using an old car mirror fixed upon the wing above his head to use as a rear-view mirror. Simple, one might think; but no one else had ever thought of it.

On the 27th July 1916 he was awarded the Military Cross for doing 'great execution among enemy planes' and 'for conspicuous gallantry on many occasions'. That same month, 66,000 British troops went 'over the top' in the biggest and most infamous infantry attack ever known, the hellish Battle of the Somme. Ball's former regiment, the 'Robin Hoods' went into action that day with 627 men. Only 90 returned. Ball was operating up above where, even from 4,000 feet, the pounding and whining of the land bombardment could be clearly heard. In the first few days of the battle, he lost eight close friends from his squadron. Master of the understatement, he told his sister in a letter, '*I am having a very poo-poo time.*'

Of his enemy he said this, '*I do not think anything bad about the Hun. He is just a good chap with very little guts, trying to do his best*'. As a patriotic put-down, it is hard to beat.

But it was his actions which spoke much louder than any words. What he did which was genuinely heroic was to take on the enemy, sometimes up to six at a time, and when he had dispatched them or sent them into turmoil, he would seek out others. Here is an example of one of his sorties undertaken just after his 20th birthday.

Having been flying all day he took off for one last duty at 7.00 pm: his task, to escort a formation of bombers over the front line. They were attacked by seven German fighters. Ball went for them, shot one down and scattered the rest. Five regrouped and returned. But there was no question of Ball making a run for it. Quite the reverse; he adopted the Ball signature manoeuvre and riddled the belly of one from only 10 yards until it exploded just in front of him, spattering his cockpit with aviation fuel. As the others attacked him, he turned directly at them and poured the remainder of his ammunition drum into the nearest until it fell away and crashed into a house 6,000 feet below. Ammunition now gone, most would call it a day; not Ball. He dived away from the enemy squadron and landed quickly at Bellevue to replenish his ammunition drums. He took off without even killing his engines and attacked the three remaining Germans immediately. He worried them to such a degree that they turned and fled. With his fuel tanks showing empty, he just cleared the front line before putting down in a field just as he ran out of gas. His windscreen was riddled with bullet holes. As a maintenance party repaired the plane throughout the night, Ball slept peacefully on the ground beside it before taking to the air immediately after breakfast. 'He was an absolute tiger for action.'*

Such superhuman displays gave Ball iconic status even at the time. Flight command told him he could fly 'as he liked'. In a slightly uncharacteristically flamboyant gesture, he had a red nose-cone fitted to the front of his Nieuport fighter, to intimidate the enemy planes. The very sight of it in the sky would frequently cause German pilots to flee in terror without engaging. The Brigadier General in command of III Brigade on the front line said, 'I'm putting your name on a big board in the trenches in order to frighten the Huns.' It was inevitable that, by September, he had been awarded the DSO for 'conspicuous gallantry and skill'. However, before he was even aware of this honour, his irrepressible fighting spirit had won him a second DSO; the swiftest brace of such medals ever awarded. But in the light of his action on the 31st August 1916, it was inevitable.

That evening he had flown over the German line at Cambrai. He saw 12 enemy aircraft forming up below him. Without hesitation he dived straight at them, scattering them before pulling-up beneath one and giving it the Captain Ball treatment from 15 yards. As it went spiralling to earth he unsurprisingly found himself under attack from the remaining 11 planes. He wove a course between them, firing at will, before his own engine was rendered useless by a burst of enemy fire into his ignition leads. Gliding and now out of ammunition, he was still undeterred and drew his pistol which he fired at the nearest opponent, taking the pilot permanently out of action. He glided so low over

* According to General Sir Peter de la Billière in his book *Supreme Courage*.

the enemy lines as he came into land that he was raked by small arms fire from the trenches.

However, quite miraculously he had shaken off his pursuers and landed safely in allied territory at Colincamp. In true Ball style, he promptly got out of his Nieuport and went to sleep beside it.

In the light of his unusual sleeping habits it is perhaps unsurprising that he was often in such a rush to be '*up and at 'em*' in the mornings that he would take-off and conduct a dog fight before returning to base, whilst still wearing his striped pyjamas. With such compulsive bravery, it was simply a matter of time before he won his third DSO for yet more conspicuous gallantry and skill, which he duly did on 25th November. With typical modesty but unquestionable pragmatism he wrote home, saying of his foe:

> '*Nothing makes me feel more rotten than to see them go down, but then you see it is either them or me.*'

At that time, the average life expectancy of a pilot on the front line was three weeks. Despite this, Ball, who would have sat totally exposed in his open cockpit, undertook hundreds of missions without receiving so much as a scratch. But if he led a charmed life, it was not to last.

After enduring a few short months posted in the UK, his persistence with Brigade Command engineered a return to the front line. It was tragic timing.

Twelve days before he left for France, he met the girl who was to be the love of his short life. Flora 'Bobs' Young was a highly attractive, 18-year-old singer working as a land-girl when Ball met her. She gave him a lift to the airfield and with that killer instinct he immediately invited her for a 'flip' in the plane. With her in her yellow dress and a borrowed flying jacket and him all smiles and dash, they must have evoked the very epitome of the age as they spun over the green patchwork of the English countryside.

But within a few days he was back in France. At his

new posting he resumed his eccentric habits, shunning the officer's quarters and building for himself a small hut instead. He established a small kitchen garden around it. In the evenings he would light a flare and walk around it in his pyjamas, playing the violin. They don't make them like Ball anymore.

Now in '56 squadron' he was pitted against one Ritt-meister Manfred von Richthofen, otherwise known as 'The Red Baron'. At this time, Von Richthofen was shooting down approximately fifteen British aircraft a month. Ball immediately set about redressing the balance. One evening he set off, cruising the skies in search of the enemy. He came upon a formation of the new German Albatrosses which he immediately attacked head-on. He shot one down and was then in hot pursuit of another. He dived so low over enemy territory to get at it that his entire fuselage was ripped apart by shrapnel from below. His plane had lost all control-wires except one. He limped home, landing with only the adjustable tail-plane to steer him. With his face covered in the oil which was still streaming from the tank, he was so angry at being put out of action that he wiped his face, ordered his other plane out of the shed and took off immediately. As is recorded by a colleague, 'within two hours he was back with yet another Hun to his credit.'

On the 7th May, the last day of his month-long posting, he took to the air with an astonishing tally of 42 German aircraft already under his belt. With Ball now in overall command of all 11 allied aircraft in his squadron, they engaged German air formations on several occasions, each time having to pull out because their Vickers machine guns jammed, a problem which dogged the pilots of the First War. Had their equipment actually worked, how different might things have been. Military kit failure is by no means only a modern-day tragedy. But those aborted attacks trig-gered the start of a dog-fight which ended in disaster. As was recorded at the time, within the setting of 'threatening masses of cumulus clouds', Ball's luck finally ran out. He was last seen by a comrade, flying at 8,000 feet into a bank of cloud in gathering darkness. He was 20 years old.

Mystery surrounds his last few seconds. From accounts of German Luftwaffe officers, he emerged from the cloud, at low level, upside down and falling for the ground. A second later he ploughed into a field by a ruined farmhouse one mile from Annoeullin. A young French woman ran to his aid and found him, still breathing in his shattered cockpit. She pulled him free, but he died in her arms. Except for a slight bruise upon his cheek, his beautiful face was untouched. For the German officers arriving shortly thereafter, it was clearly a moving scene. For such was the respect that Ball commanded from his foe that those Luftwaffe officers who retrieved his body suggested that he be shrouded in the Union Jack and dropped by parachute back behind the British line. As it was, he was buried by the Germans in the village cemetery with full military honours. His funeral came less than three months before his 21st birthday. It was a mark of exceptional respect by his adversaries, in those dark days, that he was afforded a wooden coffin.

Recreation of the last dog fight of Albert Ball
(Part of the Imperial War Museum's collection)

Subsequently, the younger brother of the Red Baron claimed to have been responsible for shooting Ball down. If genuine, in his contemporaneous account he describes Ball as 'wanting to make a fight of it to the bitter end.' That part, at least, has the ring of truth.

Ball was awarded the VC posthumously on the 8th June 1917. The formal citation included within it the following:

'For most conspicuous and consistent bravery.

In these combats, Capt. Ball, flying alone, on one occasion engaged six hostile machines, twice he fought five and once four...

On returning with a damaged machine he had always to be restrained from immediately going out on another.

In all, Capt. Ball has destroyed forty-three* German aeroplanes and one balloon and has always displayed most exceptional courage, determination and skill.'

A statue still stands of Albert Ball in the grounds of Nottingham castle.

Memorial statue to Albert Ball, photographed in 1921

* In fact, forty-four confirmed and five unconfirmed.

His father, who had started out as a plumber and ended up being the Mayor of Nottingham, was knighted for his long public service. He purchased the French field in which his son had crashed and died and there laid a plaque in memory of Albert, where it still remains. One foreign field which shall surely be forever England.

His mother never recovered from the grief of losing her beautiful boy.

Albert Ball's gravestone

ALBERT BALL: HERO PROFILE

The first ever British fighter-pilot 'ace'

Shot down at least 44 enemy aircraft

Awarded three DSOs, the Military Cross, the Legion of Honour (the highest French Order of Merit), the Order of St George (the highest military decoration of the Russian Empire) and the VC before the age of 21

Adversary of the Red Baron

Dashing, handsome and eccentric

Invented the 'rearview mirror'

Fell in love with an English rose

Died in the arms of a French girl in a foreign field

Loved by his squadron

Honoured by his enemies

Roger Bushell
'Big X'

PUBLIC SCHOOLBOY, CAMBRIDGE graduate, barrister, skier and lady-killer; Roger Bushell was the cut-glass, loveable rogue straight out of central casting. But as an RAF Spitfire pilot, escapologist and ultimately as the mastermind behind the biggest breakout from a Nazi POW camp of the entire war, he was as gritty, ruthless and irrepressible as any hero this country has ever nurtured. Though like so many, he was cut-off in his prime. Immortalised as 'Big X' in the film *The Great Escape*, Bushell represented that confident, charming yet defiant patriotism which put fire in the bellies of his fellow countrymen whilst making his enemies despair.

Born in the Transvaal of South Africa, Bushell was the son of a successful English mining engineer. The family lived in privileged surroundings, but he was no namby-pamby child. He learned to drive, ride, fish and shoot at a very early age. In fact, the Bushell family were of some antiquity, an early ancestor having fought at the Battle of Hastings as one of William's knights. In the Middle Ages, Sir Alan Bushell, who died in 1245, lived by the motto, 'While I breathe, I hope.' An older cousin of Bushell's was Major-General Orde Wingate, the inspirational leader of 'The Chindits', the guerrilla army who had the unenviable task of confronting the Japanese army in Burma during WWII. So he came from pretty brave stock.

His mother observed that as a boy he possessed two chief qualities: bravery and honesty. He was also prone to mischief. Whilst Roger was at his South African prep school, several boys were beaten for using a fire escape to spy on the matrons whilst they undressed. Whilst there is no proof that Roger was one of the miscreants, it sounds like the kind of thing he might have done. More pertinently, some also escaped from their dormitories by using the narrow heating shafts that ran down through the school to the ground floor. These shafts bear an uncanny resemblance to the inside of the famous tunnels he conceived later in his life.

At 13 he was sent to school in England: to the military academy of Wellington College in Berkshire. There he was schooled surrounded by the traditions of stiff upper lip, fair-play and gallows humour. His was an education in the Tom Brown tradition and he displayed many of the worthy characteristics of that legendary English school-boy. Despite a rebellious streak, signs that he was a born leader emerged immediately he arrived when his house-master wrote to Bushell's parents, saying:

'Don't worry about him. He has already organised the other new boys. I know the type well. He will be beaten fairly often, but he will be well liked and perfectly happy.'

Although he excelled on the sports field, Bushell was a free spirit and did not greatly enjoy the regimented life of Wellington, described at the time as 'an open prison for boys'. But he flourished and developed a suave belligerence. When he left, his house journal remembered him as an 'indomitable spirit', who was 'always prepared for anything, from big side-runs to a free fight.' When he left, he spent two terms at Grenoble University where his natural aptitude for languages was converted into true fluency in French. Being based at the foothills of the Alps placed two other new-found attractions in his path: skiing and pretty girls. These were both interests which he immediately pursued with vigour.

Rather than following his father's ambition for him, to study engineering and follow him into the mining business, Roger in fact went up to Cambridge to read Law at Pembroke College. Here he fell in with a somewhat racy set and developed what his mother perceptively described as a 'joie de vivre and a touch of joie de vice.'

Whilst he was a bright lawyer, it was his skiing that he really applied himself to. He was in the Cambridge Blues team which beat Oxford in 1930, won the Langlauf at the British Ski Championship at Wengen in 1931 and captained the combined Oxbridge team against the Canadians in 1932. It was whilst competing in Quebec that Bushell had an accident which embedded a ski-tip in his cheek and the corner of his right eye; thereafter, as can be seen from the photographs, he had a somewhat raffish, sometimes slightly sinister droop to that eye. He was described by a pioneer of Alpine skiing as 'one of the great characters of St Moritz…' An early member of the English Kandaha Club in Murren in the Swiss Alps, by the early 1930s he was 'the fastest Briton on skis'. He had a black run named after him in St Moritz, both on account of his efforts in organising Anglo-Swiss ski-meetings and, more impressively, for his smashing the record for its descent.

Having scraped through his Finals with a Third, his

friendship with the high-living Cambridge set, including Viscount Knebworth, opened the door to an even racier life as he headed for London. As his biographer, Simon Pearson described, 'The fast lane was about to become a lot faster.'

After the Great War, Lord Trenchard, the 'Father of the RAF', wished to create a reserve force of part-time pilots to act as back-up to the fledgling RAF. One of the five squadrons set up was 601 squadron, aka 'the Millionaires' on account of the type of men invited and affluent enough to join. Flying, it seems, had become the new skiing. It was an exclusive club for wealthy and well-connected young men. The admissions policy was described by an early commanding officer in this way:

'I gave each applicant marks for his school record in scholarship and athletics. And if he could ride a horse or drive a car, or a motorbike, or sail a boat or ski or play the piano, I gave him more marks.'

Lady Georgiana Curzon

It was a simple but effective way of preventing outsiders from crashing the new party. And so Bushell literally began to fly. He made up for his own relatively modest upbringing with his charm and flamboyance and by the early 1930s, Bushell was racing around London with the elite. It was through them that he met Lady Georgiana Curzon, the socialite and beauty who was to become the love of his life. They enjoyed a glorious summer in 1934. But it was not to be as, in 1935, at her parent's direction, she married the very wealthy Home Kidston.

Charm and charisma can only get you so far. Georgie's father Lord Howe had shut the door in Bushell's charming but non-aristocratic face.

Despite his great friend Lord Knebworth being killed in an air accident in 1933 – a not uncommon fate for budding pilots in those early days of military aviation – Bushell continued and loved to fly. But flying was an expensive 'hobby' and so he simultaneously embarked on a career at the Bar, in an attempt to gain some form of financial independence from his father. Bushell moved into a flat in Tite Street with an old school friend, Michael Peacock. The two were inseparable 'lads about Town'. They both flew, both practiced at the Bar and shared almost everything. They bought a car together and even shared a tail-coat between them, although one can't help but suspect that Bushell got the greater use out of both of them.

But Bushell had no need to share one thing: women. As his own sister Lis said of him many years later:

'Roger always had a girlfriend and very often a married one and a rich one. He had many, many girlfriends.'

When his own commander of 601 squadron was told that a scarlet earring had been found in the cockpit of Bushell's plane, he dryly surmised that Bushell had 'probably swallowed the other one'!

Having been called to the Bar in 1930, he showed early promise as a criminal defence advocate, practising from his chambers at 1 Temple Gardens, Middle Temple. His name appears frequently in the papers of the time. Apparently, according to one commentator, his style of cross-examination was 'as unconventional as his slalom technique'.

In 1939, just before the outbreak of war, he defended two RAF pilots for their alleged involvement in the infamous 'Battle of Barking Creek', in which a young English pilot officer was tragically shot down and killed by a British Spitfire in a chaotic, friendly-fire cock-up.

Bushell's clients were acquitted. But whatever the truth of this 'tragic shambles', the trial focussed the minds of the RAF on the inadequacies of their Radar and ID procedures at that time. This was perhaps timely, bearing in mind the imminence of the Battle of Britain.

In the meantime, Bushell had been promoted to Flying Officer in February 1934 and Flight Lieutenant in July 1936. But if the winds of war were beginning to blow across the Continent, they had not made much effect on Bushell. It was that same summer when 601 squadron 'kidnapped' an officer from rival 600 squadron, bound him and left him out on the parade ground at their base at Hawkinge airfield. When other members of the squadron rushed out to see what was lying there, Roger and his chums proceeded to bomb them from the air with bags of soot, flour and balloons filled with milk and ink. A few days later, 600 squadron retaliated when, at 4.00 am, they bombed 601 squadron at their country retreat in Kent, dropping 'bombs' of eggs, yellow ochre, rotten fruit and treacle from their 15 planes; larking about which would probably not be tolerated in the RAF nowadays.

By 1938, Bushell was selected as the volunteer pilot's representative in a show of aerobatics at the Empire Day display. As his Commanding officer described:

'His piloting, of course, was exceptional from the start…and this in a squadron where everyone was so enthusiastic and where the normal level was so high. To be outstanding in that crowd was a difficult feat.'

Meanwhile, whilst these hijinks were carrying on in good old Blighty, that same sense of humour did not seem to be replicated in continental Europe. Hitler had created a new air force and by 1937 it was dropping real bombs on real Spaniards in Madrid. On the 26th April 1937, the Luftwaffe committed what was probably the first of their countless Nazi atrocities when they dropped hundreds of bombs on the undefended town of Guernica in the Basque country, killing an estimated 1,654 civilians. The reason they did it? Target practice. By now, even Bushell and his friends, despite their japes, were starting to become aware of the imminent and ugly threat of Germany. Baldwin's government had started to expand and arm the RAF. The party was nearly over.

As news arrived of Hitler's 'deal' with Stalin to secure his Eastern Front, Bushell was on holiday in Antibes. Demonstrating typical *sangfroid*, he wrote to his parents,

> *'It's that silly ass Hitler again… it's becoming such a bore too, and what is much worse, it's mucked up my holiday this time… '*

A few days later, Hitler invaded Poland with one and a half million troops led by 1,500 Panzers. But Bushell was not intimidated, sending a short telegram to his mother: '*Don't worry. Am fighting fit. All Love. Roger.*'

With war declared on the 3rd September 1939, 601 squadron was moved from Hendon to Biggin Hill. The summer weather held as the country awaited the Luftwaffe. Roger and his crowd had hampers delivered by Fortnum and Mason and sat around, picnicking on the grass, drinking beer and playing backgammon. Aside from the outbreak of war, a chief concern for the 'Millionaires' of 601 was how to circumvent the rationing of petrol for their personal sports cars. Well, one of the gang went out and bought a local petrol station. The only problem being it had run out of petrol! Another, a member of the Guinness family 'remembered' he was, fortunately, a director of

Shell and managed to organise a delivery to fill the pumps. Friends in high places.

With fears growing of a large-scale aerial assault, Bushell was asked to form a new squadron – the first 'volunteer' to be asked. He was promoted to Leader of 92 Squadron on the 1st January 1940 and transferred to Tangmere in Sussex. When he arrived, the main snag was that there were no planes! Indeed, in the following few months of the 'Phoney War', as England desperately tried to arm itself in advance of the anticipated German attack, the vulnerabilities of the budding RAF became all too apparent. There was a gross shortage of planes. Those there were, were constantly breaking down. Pilots were in desperate need of flying experience, particularly on twin engined planes. When practice could commence, fatalities in accidents were frequent. Just as it had been for Captain Ball 20 years earlier, flying was still an exceedingly dangerous business, even without the Luftwaffe to contend with.

Bushell's 'Squadron' was then moved to Croydon. In borrowed planes, his still largely inexperienced pilots continued to suffer heavy casualties in all manner of flying mishaps. But then things took a turn for the better. Bushell's Squadron was equipped with 21 brand new Supermarine Spitfires, at the time the most sophisticated (and beautiful) fighter plane in the world. But they were infamously tricky to fly. Firstly, on take-off, the pilot had to be very careful not to let the nose dip, as the tips of the propeller passed only a few inches from the ground. Secondly, the long, shark-like nose of the engine cowling prevented the pilot having any view of the ground either on take-off or landing. Finally, in order to raise the undercarriage, vigorous pumping with the right hand was necessary, whilst simultaneously continuing to delicately control the nose and speed with the left hand. And usually all on the pilot's first solo flight; because the Spitfire only had one seat.

Bushell mastered the controls swiftly and he quickly

grew to love the sensation of flying this fast and iconic plane. His life was flying at full throttle. And with the prospect of combat only days away, he proposed to his new girlfriend, Peggy Hamilton.

And, perhaps more significantly to what followed, it must have been at about this time that he was first spoken to by members of MI9, the new agency briefed to inculcate in all servicemen, in the event of being taken prisoner, the need to gather intelligence, retain morale and, at all costs, escape. 'A fighting man remained a fighting man, whether he was in enemy hands or not.' This concept of 'escape-mindedness' led to the unwritten code that: 'It is an officer's duty to escape.' A code which Bushell adhered to until the very end.

As his biographer once again neatly summarised: 'Armed with a Spitfire Squadron, supported by British Intelligence and with a stunning new fiancée at his side, Roger Bushell was ready to go to war.'

An early Spitfire (Mark I), 1940

As Bushell began rapidly training his Squadron to fly Spitfires, Hitler invaded Denmark and Norway and the real war in the West had begun. All leave was cancelled. Churchill replaced Chamberlain as Prime Minister on the 10th May. After initial gains and the sinking of 13 major German warships, Britain started to suffer terrible losses in the bungled Norwegian campaign. Germany moved through Belgium and into the Netherlands. France was next. Churchill made his famous 'blood, tears, toil and sweat' speech in the House of Commons. 'What is our policy? I say it is to wage war. By sea, land and air.' And so it was. But it was to be a bitter start to the war. On the 20th May, his first day in command of a Squadron, Bushell's best friend from school, from London, from Chambers, Mike Peacock, was shot down and killed as he and his squadron of Hawker Hurricanes tried to halt the German advance through France. Personal tragedy was going to be something everyone was going to have to get used to.

Bushell was aware of his own and his Squadron's limitations and lack of experience. However, veteran pilots who observed him were impressed by his 'overwhelming, enveloping aura of personality and strength.' And so, with over 300,000 British soldiers stuck on the beaches around Dunkirk, Bushell did not have to be asked twice to get stuck in. On the 23rd May 1940, with the war still in its infancy, he was scrambled to lead a squadron of six Spitfires over to Calais as part of the Dunkirk evacuation. Having spotted six Messerschmitt, Bushell immediately engaged and his Squadron brought down all six German planes with the loss of only one Spitfire and pilot. In the afternoon, Bushell led another Squadron, this time of 12 Spitfires, over the French coast when he spotted an 'armada' of over 40 German fighters and bombers embarking on an attack of Boulogne. Bushell immediately gave the order to attack. He took on five of them, shooting two down before he himself was hit and his plane set on fire. Despite the engine seizing up, he managed to glide down into a field in what he hoped was friendly territory; but his luck had run out and it was with a heavy heart that he must have watched the armed German motorcycles heading straight for him. After only eight months in the RAF and on his first day of combat, he was a prisoner. For most people, that would have been the end of the war. But not for Roger.

Whilst Bushell was taken prisoner, his Squadron

presumed he, along with three other pilots lost that day, was dead. A telegram saying as much was sent to his parents. But, despite what must have been a devastating blow to morale, 92 Squadron had shot down 23 enemy airplanes on that first day of engagement. As a young pilot officer newly arrived in the Squadron remembered years later, looking back at his initial impressions of 92 Squadron and their charismatic Leader:

'He inspired a very aggressive, attacking "Let's get at 'em" attitude. They never lost it, that atmosphere. That feeling Bushell put into 92 squadron.'

Indeed, 92 squadron were to be serious a thorn in the side of the Luftwaffe over the next few years. And over the course of the war, the Squadron which the 'volunteer airman' Roger Bushell had started from scratch was to score a record 317 victories over the Luftwaffe; more than any other Squadron in the RAF. A legacy of which Bushell would have been bloody proud.

But in the meantime, Bushell and hundreds of other recently caught POWs were being forced to march approximately 350 miles towards Frankfurt, where lay Dulag Luft, the Luftwaffe interrogation centre. From there he was moved on to the camp at Stalag Luft, from where news of his survival finally reached home. In a letter to Bushell's parents, Group Captain Vincent wrote:

'We hope, most sincerely…that he is well and making such a nuisance of himself to the Hun that they will deeply regret having taken him a prisoner!'

Indeed. These were to be uncannily perceptive words. Soon after arrival, he was appointed to the permanent British camp staff under Wing Commander Harry 'Wings' Day. One of his duties was to help newly captured air crew adjust to life as a POW. The other duty was to escape. Day initially placed Bushell as deputy to Fleet Air Arm Pilot Jimmy Buckle on the escape operations committee. Later, Bushell also became head of the gathering of military intelligence, and its passing-on to MI9.

But, perhaps surprisingly, at least in the early stages of the war, the conditions in which Bushell and others found themselves imprisoned were far from barbaric. The Commandant of Stalag Luft, Major Theo Rumpel, was an Anglophile who admired the British ruling class and made great efforts to make their incarceration a tolerable one. There was little restriction on letters, books or food parcels, which the POWs could receive from friends and family all over the world. Money was earned and alcohol could be purchased. Occasional parties were permitted, some of which the Commandant would attend in person, even contributing his own whiskey ration. As Bushell himself wrote home:

> '*The stock of whiskey seems to be inexhaustible and the commandant pushes it out on the smallest excuse… !*'

Bizarrely, in the winter of 1941, Bushell was able to use his language skills and his apparent friendliness with the Germans to buy skis and go skiing in the hills, supervised by the local German officers. More extraordinary still, perhaps, was the fact that Bushell and a few of his fellow officers were occasionally invited for dinner at Major Rumpel's private cottage, beyond the perimeter of the camp. Here they would be well fed and watered and they would have hilarious evenings. But Bushell always kept his eye on the ball and continued to use his ingenuity. On the pretext of perfecting his German, he would ask the Commandant to indulge in conversational role-play; for example to pretend he was a German police officer stopping Bushell on the Swiss border! Rumpel, whether knowingly or naively, indulged him. But if he had any real fears of Bushell's imminent escape, it seems he reassured himself, saying: 'Roger, that third or fourth word was so absolutely English that even a stupid policeman would see through you.' As a fellow officer watching him in action remembered, 'Only a man like Roger Bushell could have tricked a man like Rumpel into giving him tips on how to argue his way across the Swiss frontier!'

Within a few days of this conversation in May 1941, Bushell led his first mass-breakout of the war. It had been a long time in the planning and, although not as ambitious as what followed, was an ingenious and audacious plan in itself. A long but shallow tunnel had been dug through very difficult ground. The tunnel frequently collapsed or became water-logged. It was lit by lamps which used the pure oil left from boiling margarine, with lengths of pyjama cord acting as wicks. It had been exhausting work and Bushell had done more than his fair share. But when it came to the day of the escape, Bushell decided on an alternative route which missed out the tunnel altogether. He decided to hide overnight in a tiny goat shed, along with the goat, on the outskirts of the sport's field. Once there, he only had to nip over the wire and he would be free. He would also be able to start his escape hours before the other escapees' absence was noticed and the balloon went up. In his attempt, Bushell got to within a hundred yards of the Swiss border. His journey to that point had gone seamlessly. But, with freedom almost within his grasp, he was arrested by a frontier guard and, despite the dress rehearsals with the Commandant, he was discovered. He tried to make a run for it, was shot at (but unharmed) and then taken back into custody. The 17 escapees who had used the tunnel experienced mixed fortunes. Some were re-captured almost immediately. Others got as far as Bavaria and Austria. But all were caught. On the plus side, it had led to a nationwide manhunt and diverted German troops and resources from their war effort. On the downside, it led to a tightening up of security all round, making all future attempts that much more difficult. Lessons learned on both sides, perhaps.

With characteristic chivalry, Rumpel visited many of his former charges in their new confinement. When they apologised for all the trouble they had caused him, he was good enough to admit that he would have done the same in their shoes. When Bushell finally left Frankfurt jail and boarded a coach to the next POW camp, Rumpel had left him a case of Champagne, 'With the compliments of Major Rumpel.' For his gentlemanly actions, Rumpel was 'promoted' to a job on the Polish border. The Nazi High Command did not appreciated Rumpel's sense of style, it seems.

Having been re-imprisoned in a new, purpose-built Stalag Luft I, Bushell and other German speakers adopted a new tack in their private war. With the less friendly new regime, they took to baiting the 'Goons' and trying to undermine their morale at all opportunities. This frequently led to confrontations, with Bushel using both his adversarial and linguistic skills to hold the camp regime to account. Perhaps because of this, he was moved on again, first to Lübeck and then on to Oflag VAB in Warburg. But it seems Bushell didn't much relish visiting Warburg.

En route by train, he and several others sawed through the floor of their wooden cattle-trucks and dropped out onto the rails whenever the slowing-down of the train allowed. At least one man mistimed his jump and was killed under the wheels. But Bushell and his travelling companion, Jaroslav Zafrouk – a Czech pilot who had joined the RAF and been shot down fighting over Hamburg in July 1941 – both made it. Together they got to Zafrouk's brother's farm in what had been Czechoslovakia and with his help onwards to Prague. After over 48 hours on the run, they had got to 'freedom'. It must have been exhilarating. But it was only freedom of a sort. By a stroke of rotten luck for Bushell, only days before, Prague had reluctantly received another 'tourist' in the person of Reinhard Heydrich, the psychopathic head of SS intelligence. He had been the executor of both 'The Night of the Long Knives' and 'Kristallnacht'. He was a butcher to anyone who stood in his way and subsequently was given the nicknamed 'Hitler's Hangman'. And in 1941 he had just been appointed 'Reich Protector of Bohemia and Moravia' with unlimited powers to crack down on all terrorists, resistance groups and Jews. So, the Prague that Bushell had so bravely managed to reach was a city under siege.

And things were about to get a whole lot worse. Because two undercover agents, one Czech, one Slovak, were at that very moment being parachuted into the countryside near Prague by the British. In the boldest move yet by the Special Operations Executive (aka 'The Ministry of Ungentlemanly Warfare'), their mission, scheduled for the 27th May 1942, was to shoot Heydrich: 'Operation Anthropoid'. In fact the assassination went off badly and Heydrich was only injured; but the injures were serious. They became infected and on the 4th June he died. Good up to a point. But the reprisals by the SS were unimaginably severe. Thousands were arrested. A terror engrossed Czechoslovakia. The village of Lidice, which for some reason the Nazis incorrectly suspected was linked to the assassination, was razed to the ground. Almost all of the 500 or so inhabitants, children included, were either shot, gassed or sent to concentration camps. Both of the 'British' agents, along with over 150 others who had assisted them or were believed to have been in any way connected to them, were shot. At his funeral, Himmler eulogised Heydrich as 'an ideal always to be emulated.'

But, the assassination appears to have shaken the High Command. And the 'loss' of Heydrich, one of the chief architects of 'The Final Solution', was a serious setback to the racial mass-murder previously orchestrated by Heydrich and Himmler and which was already sending thousands to their deaths on a daily basis. Up until this point, the Nazi regime had enjoyed almost only victory in its policy of aggression, invasion and suppression. After Heydrich's death, it suffered almost only defeats. Whether coincidentally or not, to that extent, it was a turning point.

But the upshot was that Bushell was trying to survive in a Prague existing in a state of terror. It was as much as he could do, with the great assistance of his friend Zafrouk and all of his Czech contacts, to stay alive and undetected. He was given shelter by the Zeithammelova family. Their daughter, Blaza, was an undercover agent for the Czech resistance. One of her friends described her as 'Blonde, voluptuous, she was a lot of fun to talk to.' I bet she was. And at 26 years old, green-eyed and athletic, it was perhaps inevitable that Bushell enjoyed 'talking to her' and they would fall for each other. By Christmas 1941, they were lovers. As one of her Czech resistance friends said, years later:

'How could they help it? He was a man. It was natural.'

Despite Bushell's supposed attachment to Peggy Hamilton back in England, perhaps Bushell couldn't help himself. In his mitigation, he had heard barely a word from his fiancée for many months. And, the emotional turmoil at being sheltered by this woman in a foreign city can only be guessed at. The excitement, fear and gratitude, after over 18 months in custody and devoid of female company, must have been overwhelming. But whether 'right' or 'wrong', wise or foolish, it turned out badly. Blaza asked for a commitment from Bushell. Bushell, being honest and thinking of home, was unable to give it to her. The relationship faltered and the expression, 'hell hath no fury...' was realised. Blaza turned to a former boyfriend, now a member of the Czech fascist party and told him of the two Allied airmen being sheltered. On the 19th May, five Gestapo officers smashed their way into the flat, seizing both Bushell and Zafouk. Incorrectly, yet ominously for Bushell, the Gestapo suspected that he was somehow involved with Operation Anthropoid.

Bushell had somewhat effortlessly defied authority all

of his life. But Gestapo HQ in Prague, in the aftermath of Heydrich's assassination, was a place where charm, arrogance or a flippant attitude will have fallen on very stony ground. One can only imagine what he had to endure. Indeed, after Prague, he was sent on for further interrogation at Gestapo HQ in Berlin where he remained for about three months. But, for whatever reason, he was finally released and sent on to Stalag Luft III, the new high-security POW camp, near the Polish border at Sagan, approximately 120 miles south-east of Berlin.

Bushell had endured months of massive personal stress. But on a personal level, Bushell had been living in something of a fool's paradise. He had been sending his fiancée Peggy Hamilton his RAF salary for over a year. The diamond engagement ring he had so thoughtfully got his father to send to her from South Africa, had arrived in London in early August of 1941. Yet months passed without hearing a word from her.

Then he had escaped to Prague. His loyalty to his fiancée had perhaps led to his arrest and interrogation. Yet, unbeknown to him, on the 14th August 1941, her engagement to Captain Lord Petre was announced in *The Times*. She had forsaken Bushell and not even had the grace to let him know. Even worse, he was to remain in the dark for over a year, by which time she had already given birth. His suspicions however, had started to surface. '*I am now beginning to wonder whether I have not been had for a sucker!*' he wrote to his parents. Indeed. However, by an extraordinary chance, his former paramour, Lady Georgie Curzon, had recently divorced *her* husband (for effectively running-off with her own step-mother!).

One door closes and another door opens. It was now Georgie Curzon to whom he directed his letters, his hopes and his love. In any event, it must have been some welcome diversion from his time at Gestapo HQ. But, the vacillations of his 'aristocratic' associates appears to have had a telling effect on him when he wrote, '*A coronet won't*

be worth much after the war anyway, which is not unfunny.'
In his letters, he never mentioned Peggy Hamilton again.

Model of Stalag Luft II, used for the film The Great Escape

The Stalag Luft III he rejoined was a far cry from the original POW camp he had been sent to two years earlier. Gone were the intimacies and fraternisation with the camp staff. But in their stead was a regime where, were a POW to wish to, he could keep his head down, study, play sports and indulge in all manner of constructive recreations. Many learned languages, took 'City and Guilds' examinations or even played golf on the camp golf-course. The prisoners were allowed to build a 500-seat theatre to put on West End musicals and plays. It was nicknamed 'The Barbed-Wire University'. On the other hand, if you wished to play cards and smoke cigarettes all day, you could.

But neither of these lifestyles were for Bushell in the long term. After he returned from Berlin he was a changed man. Gone was the levity and bonhomie with his captors. Instead, it was replaced by a deep loathing of the Germans and an almost restless desire to keep taking the fight to them. 'Grimly, quietly earnest. He was obsessed with the desire to keep on fighting them.' He had a 'clear, cool-headed hatred' which found 'sublimation in outwitting them,' was how one of his close friends described him at this time. After his Commanding Officer was transferred elsewhere, Bushell became the head of the Escape Committee. He decided that the only way to overcome the innumerable difficulties the various foiled escapes had encountered so far was to 'put the business of escaping on an industrial footing'. This was to be the X organisation; and Bushell was to be 'Big X'.

The essence and purpose of the 'Great Escape' can best be encapsulated by this extract from Bushell's inaugural meeting of the Escape Committee. Drawing on his powers of advocacy, he addressed the gathering:

'Everyone here in this room is living on borrowed time. By rights we should all be dead. The only reason God allowed us this extra ration of life is so we can make life hell for the Hun… Three bloody deep, bloody long tunnels will be dug; Tom, Dick and Harry. One will succeed!'

Ironically, for the first six months Bushell decided that they should do nothing, thereby throwing the 'goons' off the scent. But the plans continued to be hatched and Bushell had evolved into a formidable figure, who gave clear and inspirational leadership.

The plan was breathtaking in its ambition. It was to involve 600 men working on the project. It involved planning, construction, the sourcing of materials, the forging of documents, security, disposal of the diggings, intelligence and liaison. The co-ordination, discipline and organisation of such an undertaking with so few legitimate resources was indeed both an industrial and an heroic venture. And one which Bushell dealt with incredibly well. It was a masterpiece of project management. Apparently he 'had a mind like a filing cabinet'.

The plan is, of course, the stuff of legend. It was to involve the digging of three tunnels simultaneously. They were to be sunk 30 feet into the ground so as to avoid the monitors which detected vibrations in the ground. The Committee alone comprised 20 men and met on an almost daily basis. By placing all the 'bad apples' in one high security camp, the Germans had made a big mistake. They had unwittingly gathered together an unparalleled wealth of experience and expertise in escapes, tunnelling and all of its surrounding disciplines. When a covert advertisement was circulated in the camp of 1,500 men, over 1,000 volunteered to help. The expertise of these airmen covered all disciplines: surveyors, draughtsmen, tailors, electricians, carpenters, engineers, cartographers, artists, photographers, miners and mechanics. By digging three tunnels simultaneously, the venture could continue, even were one to be discovered. No German camp guard would imagine that there were more than one being dug at a time. And so, in the spring of 1943, the digging began.

The hurdles that had to be overcome may seem utterly daunting to us. Three hatches needed to be dug through solid concrete and brick, until they got down to soil level. These hatches had to be made virtually invisible. The work had to be organised into shifts, but only working when it was safe to do so. Distractions and diversions had to be set up to muffle and cover the noises of the banging. The tunnels needed lighting, ventilation and home-made 'railway' systems built into them to allow the digging to continue, transport men and equipment and evacuate the waste soil from the tunnel face. The 12½-inch gauge trolley-system was a massive advance on earlier 'sledge' systems and all the friction and wear that had entailed. It also allowed men and materials to be transported much more swiftly back and forth along the tunnel. Perhaps most ingenious of all was the invention of the bags fash-

ioned from old long woollen 'pants' which allowed the
'penguins' to disperse the excavated sand and soil, unnoticed, by emptying them out of the bottom of their trouser
legs. It must have been ingenious indeed to disperse 130
tonnes of it! To stop the frequent collapsing of the sandy
subsoil, the roofs needed to be constantly shored up. On
and on goes the list of seemingly unachievable logistics.
Their security and surveillance operation was so wide
ranging and 'official' that some German guards would even
sign-in with the duty pilots who were keeping a note of all
their movements. Indeed, it seems that the corruptibility of
the German guards was increasing as their fortunes in the
war were decreasing. A few cigarettes could buy information, tools, documents, a signature and so on.

As the official history of Stalag Luft III clearly summa-
rises:

'The ingenuity, skill, determination, team-spirit and
leadership displayed by the personnel connected with
all aspects of these undertakings is self-evident and
further comment would be superfluous.'

We should also not forget that, as well as organising the
escape, Bushell and his Senior British Officer, 'Wings'
Day, were also responsible for a mammoth counter-intelli-
gence service to MI9 back in England.

From their questioning of new arrivals and German
guards, their coded messages and network of POWs, they
were able to provide information which allowed Bomber
Command to bomb key targets in Germany, most notably
the V2 rocket HQ at Peenemunde. On 17th August 1943,
600 heavy bombers made a precision raid on the rocket
base. Although 40 bombers were shot down, the site was
destroyed. More subtly, there was a concerted and deliberate attempt to undermine German morale by the spreading
of news of increasing Allied victories and advances that
the state-controlled German newspapers did not want the

population of Germany to hear. In its own way, the very planning of the escape itself, in all of its intricate manifestations, became a kind of third front. This effect on morale did not go unnoticed. In a note by the SS from the summer of 1943, it was noted that:

'the bearing of the British is not failing to make an impression on the local population. Although a large proportion of the British prisoners come from ordinary working classes, a large number of them speak impeccable and fluent German. Their attitude is self-possessed and, indeed, often borders on arrogance. Their bearing and their whole behaviour are doubtless intended as effective propaganda.'

On it went:

'The British are the most respected and most discussed by the local population. The reason for this lies in the smart appearance of individuals. Their attitude is extraordinarily self-possessed, one could almost say arrogant and overbearing. The attitude of British prisoners to the Reich is absolutely hostile. They make fun of Germany, German institutions and leaders on all possible occasions. The manner in which the British behave to the population leaves no doubt of their confidence in victory.'

The report concludes that the very presence of British POWs in Germany was 'thoroughly demoralising'. Bushell and his men were obviously hitting their mark.

The omnipotence of Bushell and his escape committee at Stalag Luft III cannot be overstated. As one of the German guards who assisted him said in a interrogation after the war,

'At times, Squadron Leader Bushell was practically in

129

charge of the German, British and American camps [at Stalag Luft III] because nothing was done without his knowledge and approval.'

No mean achievement bearing in mind his position as a prisoner.

Of course, as we know from the Hollywood film, the audacious plan was to get 200 men in civilian clothes and with full sets of forged papers out of the camp. We know that approximately 600 POWs were involved in the plan. We know that Bushell was given the code-name Big X. The tunnels Tom, Dick and Harry commenced. One in a dark corner of a hallway. One under a drainage sump. One under a stove. Tom was discovered in August 1943 when nearing completion and all digging was suspended. But in January 1944, work resumed and on the evening of the 24th March, after months of work, 200 officers were ready for the escape.

To continue to lure the 'goons' into a false sense of security, Bushell apparently threw himself into amateur dramatics, rugby and teaching German. It was put around that he had given up the escaping game. Of course, behind the scenes, nothing could have been further from the truth. He set almost unachievable targets for his forgers, tailors, cartographers, carpenters and tunnellers.

You may ask, why did they bother? Why not, with victory if not in sight, at least nearly breaking the horizon, just sit it out? There was certainly some criticism at the time at the risks being run. But, as Bushell's biographer writes:

'for some inmates, waiting for their lives to begin again, as their wives and girlfriends took new lovers and other men took their jobs and positions at home, imprisonment became intolerable.'

They simply had to try and get home, whatever the risks.

For someone of Bushell's disposition to have spent the majority of the war incarcerated by a brutal regime must have been almost intolerable to him, and provides an insight as to why he was prepared to risk everything for the chance of escape and freedom. The humiliation of incarceration, whilst England teetered on the brink, must have made these men of action want to climb the walls, literally.

The tunnel which finally allowed the escape was so long at 345 feet that two 'halfway houses' had to be dug out to allow for men and trolleys to pass and gather. These were known as 'Piccadilly Circus' and 'Leicester Square'. By the end, the POWs' tunnelling skills had become so refined and so determined that they could dig 14 feet of tunnel a day.

Then, as if escaping was not dangerous enough already, with the passing of the Gestapo's Kugel (Bullet) Order in early March, all re-captured POWs, with the exception of British and Americans, were to be handed over to the Gestapo, by whom they would be shot. British and American would be interrogated by the Gestapo and dealt with on a case-by-case basis. 'Friendly' German guards within Stag Luft made it very clear to Bushell that, were he to be caught, with his track-record, he would certainly be shot. This decree, as well as being yet one more betrayal of the Geneva Convention, indicted the fear and annoyance such escapes were causing.

But it did not intimidate Bushell for a moment. Nor many of the other men. Of the 600 who had worked on the escape, 500 applied to be part of the breakout, even though 'only' 200 could be chosen to actually escape. The digging pressed on more fervently than ever. Within 10 days of the Bullet Order, tunnel Henry had reached its end and a vertical shaft had been dug, finishing just nine inches beneath the surface. The 'Great Escape' was on.

The first 30 places were reserved for the fluent German speakers who, it was considered, had the best chance of making it home. Being out of the tunnel would give them those precious few extra minutes of advantage before the balloon went up. The names were drawn by ballot. Bushell was number 4. Each escaping POW was provided with a kit of clothes, documents, tools and rations; maps, money, identity cards, compasses; hats, bags, overcoats, books, letters. Everything which, at least on a cursory inspection, would make the escapee appear to be a legitimate member of the public. Some were to travel as businessmen; some as workers; some as French; some by passenger train. Some by worker train. Some on foot. Each had a tailor-made and well rehearsed cover story. Bushell performed interviews on every one of the other 199 escapees.

Perhaps the excitement within the camp was palpable; with the escape imminent, the Commandant of Stalag Luft commented that one of the most intractable security problems he faced was the '*esprit de corps* prevailing particularly within the British Air Force.' And wholly in keeping, within a few days, Bushell delivered a stirring 'eve of battle' speech. One POW from the Parachute Regiment remembers that, at that moment, 'he had the camp behind him to a man.' But they all knew what they were facing. When Bushell was challenged that escaping now, in snow and bitterly cold weather, didn't give those on foot much chance, he replied, '*They haven't got much chance anyway.*'

Of course, there was a litany of last-minute logistical details to sort out. But most importantly, the night for escape needed to be cloudless. The documents needed to reflect the correct date. It could not be a Sunday as the train timetables would be very limited. And so the date was set for the Friday night, 24th March 1944. Despite the fact there was still snow on the ground, ultimately Bushell decided: '*We go tonight.*'

Infuriatingly, after all that work, the surveyors had somehow misjudged the distance and the tunnel emerged just 10 feet short of the dark cover of the pine forest. That was not the only hurdle they faced at the last minute. Ironically, because of a bombing raid on Berlin, there was a general blackout, plunging the tunnel and the nearby town of Sagan into blackout. There was a small tunnel collapse which needed to be repaired before more men could get out. But a short discussion and a system of rope and signals was set up to allow each prisoner to escape without being spotted by the guards. As the first men emerged, it was a clear night and they could see the stars above them. The words of the RAF motto must have come to mind: '*Per ardua ad astra*', 'Through endeavour to the skies'. Bushell was in the first 20 out. They assembled in the woods. They then all made for Sagan railway station in twos and threes. There was a train at 11.00 pm that night. The time was now just after 10.15.

Despite the skill and ingenuity which had gone into making the various outfits and disguises, the men were noticed at the station. A censor at the Stalag Luft sorting office noticed several men, strangely dressed, hanging around the station as she emerged from the cinema in Sagan. She tipped-off the station policeman, who checked their documents, but fortunately concluded that they seemed to be in order. When she got back to the camp, she enquired as to whether there had been any unusual activity at the camp and was told that, no, all was quiet. It was just about the only bit of luck they had that night.

Meanwhile, whilst the first wave boarded the 11.00 pm train to Breslau, things were not going well in the tunnel. Some were trying to take too much kit. Others had knocked into supports, causing tunnel collapses. The whole process was slowing down. It became clear that all 200 men were never going to be able to escape. As dawn approached at 5.00 am, it was decided that man number 87 was to be the last man out of the tunnel. Then, at about that time, a prison guard veering from his normal beat, saw figures in the woods. A shot was fired and within seconds, the game was well and truly up. The tunnel was quickly evacuated.

Papers were burnt. Kit hidden. Pandemonium broke-out amongst the camp guards. Shouting. Running.

At Breslau railway station, where several escapees had by now arrived, they heard an announcement over the station tannoy calling for the station master, head of security and the police. It was approaching 6.00 am. Bushell was there. These must have been agonising moments.

But despite the alarm having been raised, Bushell and his French travelling companion were able to buy tickets for and board the Paris train.

Meanwhile, back at Stalag Luft, the camp Commandant had been informed. He was apoplectic with rage. Four heavy machine guns were pointed at the prisoners' barracks. The rooms were searched. One of the 'ferrets' was sent down from the exit of the tunnel and finally emerged in Hut 104. The prisoners were turned out of the hut and ordered to strip in the snow. The atmosphere must have been icy. Yet, despite that, four of 'our boys' showed enough defiance to be sent to 'the cooler': one for mocking the Germans and another, commendably, simply 'for laughing.'

Despite the meticulous planning, 'only' 76 of the 200 escapees made it clear of the camp. But it was still the biggest break-out of the entire war. And it had the desired effect on the German High Command.

Despite Germany retreating on all fronts, despite the suspected and imminent Allied invasion of Europe, the 'Great Escape' went right to the top of Hitler's in-tray. He was not happy. If Bushell's ambition was to '*make life hell for the Hun*' and to sap their morale, then surely this is the moment when he achieved his goal. To have seen Hitler's expression as the news reached him would have been priceless. With a visceral out-lashing of bitterness, rage and humiliation, he ordered that all escapees were to be handed over to the Gestapo and shot. In fact, for some arbitrary reason, the number to be shot was then modestly reduced to 50. But that is perhaps a nicety. The upshot was that Hitler personally gave the order to murder 50 Allied prisoners of war.

The very epitome of being a bad loser.

It was Himmler who was left to work out the practicalities which, no doubt, he did with glee.

'The shootings will be explained by the fact that the recaptured officers were shot whilst trying to escape, or because they offered resistance, so that nothing can be proved later.'

The Nazis well knew the deliberate and egregious malice of their actions.

The selection of the '50' appears to have been wholly arbitrary. Young and old, from all nationalities. Some of the most troublesome prisoners, for some reason, were spared.

But Bushell was still at large and approaching Saarbrucken by train, some 500 miles from Sagan, and so nearly into French Alsace. But then they were stopped by two German 'Kripo' policemen. One of the escapees inadvertently answered a question in English. Their papers were checked by a policeman. He was unsure of their authenticity and they were detained. They had run out of road. It was the 29th March 1944, just two months or so short of D-Day.

Bushell and his companion Scheidhauer were split up. They had no choice but to accept their true identities. Initially Bushell was well treated. Given cigarettes and food. But then things changed. He was transferred to the Gestapo. Two officers in those sinister Black SS uniforms handcuffed them and told them to get in the back of the car.

These men were a Dr Leopold Spann and an Emil Schulz. Bushell, sensing that things had taken a serious turn for the worse, told them in German that their conduct was incompatible with the honour of being an officer. But it was pearls before swine. He was told they were simply following orders. They were driven along the Autobahn between Homberg and Kaiserslautern. The car pulled off the road. They were ordered out of the car. Spann and Schultz got out with them, pistols in hand.

It took two shots to kill Bushell. One to the back of the head. A second to the temple as he lay, convulsing on the ground. Murder in cold blood. All over Germany, the remaining 49 were rounded up individually and in small groups. And, one by one, on the verges and lay-bys, in the back streets and the woods of Central Europe, they were murdered. Although the official story related to the various POW camps around the country was that they had been shot trying to resist arrest or whilst trying to re-escape, when Group Captain Herbert Massey asked the new commandant, 'How many had simply been injured?' the chilling answer was, 'None.' And, in so doing, the Nazis committed the greatest crime of the war against British servicemen. All of the men were in their 20s and 30s.

Those who chance favoured and survived included the Senior British Officer at Stalag Luft, 'Wings' Day. Perhaps even the Nazis baulked at the repercussions were such a senior and well-known officer to be executed. The last of the Great Escapers died, aged 99, as recently as February 2019. Dick Churchill, a bomber pilot, always suspected his life was only spared execution on account of his surname. If so, a very fortuitous coincidence for him.

On the 19th May 1944, the news of this atrocity was delivered in the House of Commons by Anthony Eden, the Foreign Secretary. Shortly after, having dismissed Germany's feeble attempts to explain these deaths and referring to the Gestapo officers who carried out the murders, the following statement was read to The House:

'His Majesty's Government must, therefore, record their solemn protest against these cold blooded acts of butchery. They are firmly resolved that these foul criminals shall be tracked down to the last man wherever they may take refuge. When the war is over, they will be brought to exemplary justice.'

Immediately after the war, a team of RAF investigators embarked on a three-year quest to track down the perpetrators. They were tenacious. In the end they identified 72 of the Germans involved. Eleven committed suicide. Six had been killed in the last few months of the war. But 38 of them were finally tried. Seventeen of them were imprisoned; and 21 executed.

Bushell's murderer Emil Schultz was one of those tried. After the trial, his wife and two daughters appealed to the Royal Family for clemency. Their plea was refused. Rightly, you may well think. No doubt, to his own family, Schultz was a decent man, who simply found himself in the wrong place at the wrong time. But, there again, the same might be said of Roger Bushell. And, to use a phrase, 'what goes around comes around.'

Three men did escape, however. Jens Muller and Per Bergsland, Norwegian pilots made it back to Britain, via Sweden to continue the fight. As did a Dutchman, Bob van der Stock, having reached the Pyrenees and eventually Gibraltar.

Sadly, but inevitably, the generally benign Commandant of the camp and a dozen of his staff were courtmartialled. Perhaps understandably, in the course of their trial, the military prosecutor was somewhat perplexed and anxious to know how it was, for example, that the prisoners had been loaned a camera? How a huge 200-metre drum of electric cable had 'gone missing' without rousing any suspicion? At a time when Germany was desperate for resources itself, perhaps the incredulity of the Court martial tribunal is understandable when they learned that, amongst other things, during the 15 months leading-up to the escape, the POWs has managed to 'borrow':

1,699 blankets
3,424 towels
62 tables,
90 double beds
2279 knives, forks or spoons
and 30 shovels.

You can see why, when the tunnel was discovered, one of the prisoners couldn't help but laugh at the Germans.

A week later, on the 8th June, Bushell was mentioned in despatches for his herculean efforts.

Inexplicably, despite being recommended for a post-humous George Cross by intelligence chiefs after the War, the 'War Office' turned him down. The dead hand of the civil service as alive and kicking then as it is now...

By the time of his murder in 1944, Bushell's parents were living in the small town of Hermanus in the Cape Province. They heard about his death on the radio. The final letters he had written them from Stalag Luft III continued to arrive in the weeks after the war had ended. It must have been agonising. Bushell's cousin Orde Wingate was also killed in an air crash the same month that Roger died. Roger's mother never got over the loss of her golden boy. For years afterwards, 'she lived upstairs, in her own world,' her granddaughter remembers.

Likewise the other great love of Roger Bushell's life, Georgie Curzon. For years after the war, she could not come to terms with the fact he was never going to return. Then, once she accepted the reality, every year she would put a notice in *The Times* on his birthday, the 30th August, and she did so many times during the 1940s and 50s. Eventually, encouraged so to do by Bushell's parents, she moved on and married. But she died quite young, aged 66. On her tombstone read two lines of Tennyson, which, one can't help but think, must have harked back to Roger:

'Oh for the touch of a vanished hand,
And the sound of a voice that is still.'

Although Roger Bushell never attended the school in Hermanus, South Africa, where his parents retired, it is a mark of the man that every year the local school still awards two prizes in his name: one for mastery of foreign languages, the other for sheer force of character.

Bushell Green in Bushey, London, is named after him. His name rests on the Memorial Board at Wellesley House, Wellington College and on a bronze plaque in Chapel Cloister, Pembroke College, Cambridge. And the 'Bushell Run' still remains at St Moritz, albeit now inaccessible and hidden within an area of protected woodland. Whether that would stop Roger still skiing it, is another question...

Despite the Gestapo's attempts to make him and his friends 'disappear' all those years ago, the names of 'The 50' all remain, bold as brass, immortalised on their memorial which stands upon the site of their escape, just outside the North Compound of Stalag Luft III. This time, it was to be a corner of a foreign forest that shall remain forever England.

The '50' memorial

Roger Bushell is buried in Poznan Old Garrison Cemetery. And as well as the memorial to 'The 50' which stands at

139

Sagan, in 2017 a further memorial was erected, marking the very spot on which some of the 50 were murdered, just outside Ramstein Air Base in what is now, and always really has been, Poland.

Bushell has been immortalised on film, both by Ian McShane in *The Great Escape II, The Untold Story* and, of course, by Lord Dicky Attenborough in his iconic portrayal of 'Herr Bartlett' in *The Great Escape* itself.

He may have felt that he 'missed out' on the War and all of its danger, opportunity and vitality. But *he* created one of its enduring stories and has achieved an immortality which he could never have imagined and which, undoubtedly, would have brought a raffish smile to his sensuous lips and a twinkle in that slightly hooded eye... Irreverent, mischievous and defiant to the end. My God, how the Nazis would have hated it.

As his simple epitaph so succinctly puts it:

'A leader of men, he achieved much, loved England and served her to the end.'

ROGER BUSHELL: HERO PROFILE

Had a ski run named after him

Went to Cambridge

Had loads of girlfriends

One of the best pilots of his generation

Set up a Spitfire Squadron which shot down more German planes than any other. Ever

Helped our boys escape from Dunkirk

Survived interrogation by the Gestapo

Escaped from a German POW camp three times

Masterminded the biggest break-out of the entire War

Had one of the most famous films of all time made about his exploits

Made Hitler very angry

Made the Germans look stupid